So many books are written about the young, beautiful and rich people falling in love in some kind of pseudo-fantasy world that most of us can't identify with. That's why I find it refreshing to read a story like this one about Peter and Linda. I love stories about being given a second chance, especially for love.

The characters are older, scarred by life physically and emotionally; one living much like you would expect a lonely traveling salesman's life to, and the other a dutiful wife in a loveless marriage. You can imagine all the scenarios that this combination can promise, as in any good story. The author brings his own peculiar style and bank of knowledge in the telling.

I would recommend this trilogy to anyone wanting to settle back and enjoy being with a thoughtful man's complicated pursuit of a lost love. Peter's determination made me root for him to win Linda. I hope you'll discover what I did—that love can be a gentleman.

—Margaret Carson, Pastor's Wife, Lawrenceville, GA

I don't typically like to read because it puts me to sleep, but not Al's book. I didn't want to sleep, I just wanted to keep reading. I could just see myself in that deer stand doing the same things, this gave me great laughter. Oh yes, I remember my first *Dear Love*... Then there were the tears of joy and sadness. It left me ready for more of what the future will bring in the next story. Thanks Al for my fond memories, laughter, excitement and tears.

—Patsy Gray, Retired Businesswoman, Eatonton, GA

The Deer/Dear Hunt series is well written. You can't wait to get to the next chapter to see what will happen next. There is suspense, drama, comedy and love all rolled into one wonderful read. Mr. Oberdeck gives you the feeling that you are personally involved with many of the characters.

It is almost as if you know the characters personally and can feel their emotions. When you finish reading *The Deer/Dear Hunt* you feel that there should be a sequel to this series. It is a very easy read and hold's you interest throughout the entire series.

—Jim and Lucinda Spicer, Eatonton, GA

Young sweethearts grow old and look back on their memories of what might have been, if they had married each other—that is the love theme of this trilogy. They now have a second chance to let their renewed love blossom into the marriage they missed with each other. It is not as easy as they dreamed it would be; but as the song goes, "Ain't Love Grand?"

—Jim and Joy Fason, Retired Missionaries to India, Eatonton, GA

THE DEER/DEAR HUNT

BOOK 1

A SALESMAN'S GUIDE TO HUNTING

ALAN M. OBERDECK

Inquiries and Book Orders should be addressed to:

Great Writers Media
Email: info@greatwritersmedia.com
Phone: (302) 918-5570
24A Trolley Square #1580 Wilmington, DE 19806-3334, USA

ISBN: 978-1-961416-00-0 (sc)
ISBN: 978-1-961416-01-7 (ebk)

DEDICATION

I wish to dedicate this book to all the salesmen I have traveled with who, during the long drives between calls, on occasion took a break with me from talking business to listen to some of my story ideas and ramblings.

CONTENTS

PREFACE

I was born and raised in southern Wisconsin on a farm near Edgerton. When I was twelve years old, I contracted the polio virus. It forever changed the direction of my life from wanting to escape from the farm and go to California on a motorcycle to deciding to pursue becoming a Lutheran minister. The Lord had other plans, though, and I became a salesman and eventually a regional manager working with other salesmen. I learned a lot about life from the men I traveled with.

In *The Deer/Dear Hunt*, I have tried to explore four threads and, from my experience, weave them together into an intriguing story. The threads are: 1) Can you ever go back home? 2) The far-reaching effects of a life-changing accident. 3) The deep-seated memory of a first love. 4) The deep, internal conflict felt by those involved. These threads had an appeal to many of the men I traveled with and many I have known since. They form the platform for an unusual love story. In this story, I have tried to pattern the human nature and actions of many of the characters after Christian people I have known.

I chose to have Peter Waldmann be a successful salesman. I tried to portray Peter as an ethical, stiff, conflicted, and anal-retentive salesman relying on his routine to survive. I wrote the book as though Peter were writing daily and weekly sales trip reports. I chose Edgerton, Wisconsin, as my setting because of my familiarity with the area, and I actually went deer hunting there in the weather described in the book. All the roads depicted in the story are there and can be found.

INTRODUCTION

It is Saturday night, and I've just finished the opening day of this deer-hunting season. Basically, I'm not much of a sportsman, much less a hunter, and not at all experienced in the art of deer hunting. Actually, I'm an animal lover sharing my home with a number of cats and a very friendly watchdog. To make a living, I sell things—specifically, Capital Equipment—but that doesn't give any clue as to why I've just spent a day deer hunting.

It all started several months ago when I made a sales call on one of my accounts near Savannah, Georgia, only to find out that my contact had been promoted and I was to meet his replacement. I cooled my heels in the lobby for the appropriate amount of time. Eventually, the door opened, and Sarah, his secretary, ushered me into the office of the new buyer.

As I walked in, I was greeted with, "Peter Waldmann! When Sarah gave me your card, I never in my life thought it could be you. I thought you were up North someplace!"

"John Stemple," I said in surprise. I didn't know at first what to say. Meeting him here took me totally by surprise.

Now, in the sales business, you are treated to surprises almost daily; however, the really big surprises come only rarely. Well, this was one of those really big ones! The buyer I met was John Stemple, someone I hadn't seen since I was a junior in high school. In fact, at that time, he was my closest friend.

We talked about the product lines I represented and the products I usually sold to his company. We talked about what we had done since the last time we had written to each other. I invited him to go to lunch with me. During lunch, he told me about his family and his move to Savannah. He was currently staying in a motel, but had bought a house, and his family would be moved-in in a couple of weeks. We reminisced a little about growing up together. One thing led to another, and he invited me to come home with him to go deer hunting over the Thanksgiving holidays.

Home, as he called it, was a little town in southern Wisconsin named Edgerton, situated halfway between Madison and Beloit, right where Highway 51 and Highway 59 cross. He was raised on a farm near there. I spent some of my formative years there. If you could find Edgerton in a tourist information book today, it would read:

"Edgerton, WI: a quaint town of approximately five thousand, situated in the midst of a lush farming area noted for its production of milk, grain crops, and leaf tobacco. The low, rolling hills and valleys are crisscrossed with a patchwork of tree-lined farm fields, hardwood forests, and roads dotted with unique old farm buildings. The town boasts many antique and craft shops. It still has many tobacco warehouses dating to the turn of the century, when it was lovingly called Tobacco City. Among the sights that might interest some are the factory buildings of the old Highway Trailer Co. and the old Edgerton Shoe Factory, both of which played an active part in the WWII war effort. The main recreation area is Lake Koskonong, the second largest lake in Wisconsin. The summer tourist season lasts from Memorial Day to Labor Day and is highlighted by a midsummer festival called Tobacco Days."

In all my looking, though, I never found Edgerton featured in any tour guide, but I did find Lake Koskonong.

So here I am sitting in a motel in Janesville, Wisconsin, fourteen miles away from the hunting land, having hunted deer all day on a farm near Edgerton.

The original plan was for John to drive from Savannah to my place in Lilburn, Georgia, on the Thursday morning of the week before Thanksgiving and prepare for the hunting trip. This preparation was to include my buying the right kind of gun with which to hunt and to become properly outfitted for the weather we would encounter. We would then leave early Friday morning to drive to our base of operations, the Holiday Inn Express motel in Janesville, Wisconsin. We planned to arrive early that evening. We would then hunt for nine days on a farm near where he had grown up. The arrangements were all made. I bought my out-of-state deer license. I was ready for my first serious deer-hunting trip!

Two days before the trip was to begin, the phone rang.

"Hello?" I answered.

"Hi!" said John Stemple. "I have some problems that will keep me from driving to Lilburn on Thursday."

"Is your family all right?" I asked nervously.

"Nothing like that," he answered. "The first sample of the raw materials I am buying isn't up to specs. I have to take a trip out to visit the supplier. I don't know my schedule right now, but I won't be able to drive to Lilburn on Thursday."

"That's too bad," I answered. I didn't know what to say. This was a somewhat sudden change of plans. I thought to myself, *The easiest thing to do would be to cancel the trip.*

Before I could say anything, John said, "Now here is what I want you to do: I plan to be up as soon as I put this to bed. The latest should be Thanksgiving Day. You go right on up Friday, and when the season opens on Saturday morning, claim the deer stands," John instructed.

"John, I haven't been back there in forty years! I'll get lost! Remember, I was a town kid and never did much roaming in the country," I countered.

"Pete, old man, nothing much has changed back there in the last forty years. Besides, I'll draw you a map from the motel in Janesville to the area where the stands are and fax it to you," he replied.

"I've never hunted much, let alone in the dark! I don't even have a gun. Besides, how will I know when the season opens on Saturday?" I rather naively asked.

"First, go to a sporting goods store at the mall, and they will tell you what gun you need. Then go to a shooting range and practice. Now, how will you know when hunting season starts? Two ways: first, look at your Wisconsin State Hunting Guide, and read the official time the season opens on the first day; but you will know without even looking," he said with a laugh. "When the gunfire around you reminds you of the TV news from the war in Bosnia, you will know the time has come and the season is open."

"You're kidding, of course."

"Have a good time. I will be up with you as soon as I can," John said as he hung up the phone.

I thought about this news and immediately called Delta Airlines to find the cheapest plane fare from Atlanta, Georgia, to someplace close to Edgerton. The best connection with the best fare was to fly to Chicago and rent a car. I called Hertz and reserved my rental car for the ten days I would be there. This insured I would have my own wheels, even when John joined me, and not be stranded.

I went to a sporting goods store near Gwinnett Place Mall and bought a twenty-gauge Winchester pump shotgun and shotgun slugs, to comply with the hunting rules in Rock County WI. There was a shooting range near there where I could fire it, and I tried it out. One of the salesmen had given me the rudimentary instructions as to how to aim and such. I bought the proper container for the gun so I could check it as luggage for my flight to Chicago. While at the sporting goods store, I bought the orange hat and vest so I could be seen while hunting and considered myself set for this great adventure.

I flew up on Friday afternoon, picked up my Hertz Sable, drove the Illinois Tollway to Beloit, stopped to eat at a Beloit exit, and was safely in the Janesville Holiday Inn Express motel and in bed by 9:00 p.m. Early to bed and early to rise gets the deer hunter in the field an hour before sunrise, *so when the deer come around they do not notice you*, I reasoned. If you believe this is true, I, a salesman of Capital Equipment, have some land I want to sell you right on a government preserve in Georgia!

Sunrise was to be at or around 6:30 a.m. Well, being from an earlier time zone, getting up early enough to be safely in the field by then did not seem like much of a stretch. When I arrived at the stand, I couldn't read my watch in the dark, so I decided to take John's advice and listen. He had said, "When the gunfire reminds you of the TV news from the war in Bosnia, you know the time has come." I was skeptical, but suddenly, the gunfire started and continued for about five minutes. I wondered if there would be any deer left; but I am getting ahead of my story.

I awoke at 4:30 a.m. and immediately got dressed. Of course, being from the sunny South, I did not have a closet full of the proper clothing. John had planned to help me in this regard, but seeing that he was not there to help, I chose to improvise by layering my clothes. I was not practiced at pulling so many layers of clothing over one another, so I went through a dressing ritual befitting someone planning to visit the Arctic.

Eventually, heavily layered and stiff from all the clothing, I went over to the window in my room and pulled back the drape. Through the window, I saw what I had heard every deer hunter dreamed of: snow! The snow on the ground appeared to be at least two inches deep, and the snow was still falling. I could see the outline of the roads, but none of them were plowed clear yet. Naturally, I was a bit excited. Well, maybe more than just a bit.

I spoke to the motel desk clerk as I left the lobby on my way to the Sable. I guess I was quite a sight, as he was much amused. After making some comments about straightjackets and being stuffed like a scarecrow, he wished me good luck during my first day on the hunt. His laughter and comments belied his encouraging words that followed me as I left the lobby.

Tramping through the snow on the way to my car, the cold, wet realization the snow was becoming deeper than the height of my slipover rubber galoshes finally struck home. The wet snow was spilling over the sides of my galoshes into the sides of my oxford shoes. I would be sitting on an elevated stand in a snowstorm with wet feet, wet trouser legs, wet posterior, and wet anything else not covered by water-repellent material.

I stopped at the quick stop near the motel and picked up coffee and a sweet roll for my breakfast. I got back in the Sable and turned on the overhead map light so I could read the directions John had faxed to me. I drove out of the street the motel was on and made a left turn onto Highway 14. I followed it west to Highway 51. I turned right on Highway 51 and headed north toward Edgerton. The motel was located on a flat area of what could be called the Rock River Flood Plain. As I drove north, the road began to rise and fall as it followed the contour of the gently rolling hills. I turned left onto County M at the farm buildings John had marked on the map to take the road to Indian Ford. County M started out on what could have been part of the flat flood plain, but it slowly dropped in altitude to above-river level as it entered Indian Ford. I crossed the bridge at what he had marked as the Rock River and observed the dam to my left.

After driving up and down low hills and around gentle curves with my visibility impaired by the falling snow, I crossed another bridge. *I must be lost*, I thought. *This river does not appear on my map.* Nothing looked familiar in this snow. All of a sudden, I came to a crossroad with houses and some other buildings visible through the snow. I was in the little village marked "Fulton" on my map. The decision to turn right on the road marked 184 was easy, as continuing straight didn't look promising. By now, my vague memories of this area were beginning to come to the surface.

Even after having been away for forty years, I began to recognize the village of Fulton. Things had changed. Someone seemed to be living in what had been Murwin's Grocery Store. The electric generating station that had been on the river where I fished with John was nowhere to be found; I couldn't even find the millrace that fed it. I thought I remembered two bridges leaving Fulton, but I only crossed one. I continued on Highway 184, up and down the same gently rolling hills. I looked again at the map and saw a curve at the junction with Highway 59. I followed 184 around that curve and ended up heading west on 59. Finding this cleared my confusion, and I easily located the driveway along the right-hand side of the road onto the field where we were to park the car.

The sky was dark; visibility through the falling snow was only about twenty feet when I carefully parked the car. I went to the trunk and unsheathed my shotgun. I followed the description from John's map: "Walk straight back from the car to the fence. At the fence, turn to your left, and follow the fence to the stand. From your stand, you should see the fence that makes the corner of the field." I followed his instructions and found my way through the snow to the stand. It was a short walk, but as I walked, I picked up more and more snow in my shoes. From the stand, through the heavy snow, I could vaguely see the fence at the corner.

As I looked up to the top of my stand, a ladder with a flat perch nailed to it leaning precariously against a tree, it reminded me of the lookout platform I had been on at the top of the rigging of a three-masted sailing vessel I once visited. One thing, though, was obvious when I reached the top: I had to sit.

I checked my pocket one more time for the location of the five slug shells for the shotgun. I carefully held the gun in one gloved hand while I climbed the ladder using the other hand for support. When I reached the platform, I found when I tried to stand it was very unstable. The sky was still dark, and the visibility through the falling snow now seemed less than before. I knew there were other stands somewhere out there, but I had no idea where.

I attempted to brush as much snow as possible from the flat surface of the platform, but when I sat on the surface, there was enough snow left for my body heat to melt and make the seat of my trousers wet. The heat from my hand was now melting the snow on my one glove, making it wet. Now there I sat, legs dangling over the edge of the platform. They were too short to reach one rung of the ladder and unable to be supported on the slippery next rung up.

It seemed safer to me not to load the gun until I was safely up in my perch. Now the gun lying across my lap was trying to obey the rather stringent laws of gravity while my bare fingers, wet with the falling snow, were rapidly being frozen stiff. All this while I tried to slip the five slug shells into the shotgun receiver. I never did find the one shell I dropped. I felt as though I was sitting on a wet, unstable, slippery block of ice somehow suspended above a layer of white clouds. I sat and waited.

What does one do while sitting like a bird on a perch awaiting the arrival of the ubiquitous deer anyway? When I had speculated about this earlier, I assumed this might be similar to fishing. Both are sports requiring patience, silence, alertness, and the luck of being at the right place at the right time. But, here and now, I noticed great differences. If you fish in the cold, you sit in a warm fishing shanty away from the cold. You don't sit in an open boat in a snowstorm! You throw the line in the water with a baited hook attached and try to get the fish to bite. You can even use a fish finder.

On the other hand, when hunting deer, you sit, stand, or squat out in the open, wearing orange clothing, hoping some blind deer will wander close enough to where you are to be shot at. You are not allowed to use bait!

Still, in both sports, you do need patience to sit there and the ability to remain alert enough to react when the fish bites or the deer wanders too close.

It seemed like there was still a long time before sunrise, and something had to be done to stay awake. Mental activity usually will keep me awake. As I sat there trying to warm my hands, waiting for the hunt to begin, my mind began to wander to the long-forgotten memories of my youthful sojourn in Edgerton.

Memories to Keep Me Awake

My family moved to Edgerton when I was in fourth grade. My father had gone to college on a work/school program sponsored by General Motors and had spent the war years working in one of the wartime production plants for GM in the Chicago area. At the end of the war, GM moved many of these young engineers around the corporate system. My dad was transferred to the Fisher Body plant in Janesville, Wisconsin. For reasons I can never understand, Mom wanted to live in a town much smaller than Janesville. For some reason, they choose Edgerton. I transferred into the Edgerton grade school system at the beginning of my fourth-grade year. I remained in that system through my junior year in high school, but that is getting ahead of the story.

A boy entering a new school system, having come from a system as sophisticated as those on the West Side of Chicago had been in the late forties, was in for a little culture shock. First of all, no one knew me. That was not all bad. Secondly, I had to make friends with the boys in the class. Thirdly, they had a pecking order that I correctly identified and understood. Fourthly, having been pretty high on the pecking order where I came from, I was not inclined to start on the bottom with this one. It was while this rearranging of these important things in my life was taking place that John and I became best friends.

Of course, there were other things that happened at that time that also played heavily on my future happiness. It seemed those boys further up the pecking order than you were more interesting to the prettier girls in the class. Now, when I was that age, heaven help the person who came up to me and accused me of liking a particular girl! That was not done without retribution. There would be an almost immediate fight that would end when one boy was pinning the other to the ground and trying to get him to "take that back."

Unfortunately, the teachers didn't understand that aspect of the youthful exercise of testosterone. The fight usually was ended by a teacher doling out hours and hours of recess detention or eraser cleaning after class. Knowing that I came from Chicago, the teachers were very critical of my schoolyard behavior. Many times, this gave me the opportunity to improve my penmanship by copying pages of dictionary during the recess period.

It was during fourth grade that I discretely became friends with the girl who could be referred to as my soul mate. The hours of eraser cleaning and dictionary copying precluded my becoming friendly with this special person during recess periods at school. In the beginning, not having recess caused me some concern. In the long run, being out of contention for her favors out on the schoolyard was good. I never had to fight over her, and we never became that much of an item.

It is interesting now as I think about it. Here I was, sitting in an uncomfortable position, becoming colder and wetter by the minute, yet, from deep in my memory appeared the one warm spot I had in my heart for this place, and it was this girl. I remember her name was Linda Leigh Swensen, and, with the thought of her name, the memories flooded back.

I was just beginning to think about how we met when my thoughts were interrupted by the sound of distant shots from my right. *Well, John was right on about this one*, I thought. Here the sun is coming up on a snowstorm, the deer can't be seen unless they have ventured to within at least twenty feet of my stand, and already someone has shot at something. Then I heard an answering volley from my left. Those had just died away and then more shots from my right and then from behind. At this point,

I heard the *zing, zing, zing* of a slug passing somewhat over my head close to my left side.

Well, I thought, *either he missed, or the slug went right through that deer.* Then a second thought hit me: *Here I am perched up here with the possibility of bullets zinging all around me! Am I crazy?*

The next thought, though, was a little more rational: *How many hunters are out here, and where the heck are they?* It was then I began to look through the falling snow for the orange vests and caps that silently cried out *Human inside! Don't shoot*! The shooting around me continued, but fortunately, I heard no more close bullets.

Now I know what John was talking about when he said, "When the gunfire reminds you of the war in Bosnia on TV you will know the time has come."

Now that it was light out, I could see more through the falling snow and get my bearings. My stand was facing south across the field toward Highway 59. There was a small knoll in front of me, rising slightly as it approached the fencerow to my right. As the knoll became a hill, it crossed the fencerow and became a wooded area. My stand leaned against a larger tree along a brushy fencerow. John's stand was farther down the fencerow to my left, positioned similarly to mine. As I sat facing Highway 59, looking over this field of unbroken, white snow, the beauty of the area momentarily took my mind away from the cold that was penetrating my body. At my back was another field bordered by small, wooded hills on two sides. I turned to look at the field. It was a rather long field that ended at a forest that appeared to be bordered by a natural fence of shrubbery. The shrubbery continued to follow the contour of the hill until it intersected with the fence that became the eastern border of the field. The side that was open was to my left as I faced north toward the wooded area. Looking through the falling snow now in the light of day, I could see that across the bushy fencerow to my right and continuing to the south at the edge of wooded area were more snow-covered farm fields.

More shots rang out. *Calm down*, I told myself. *If these guys have to shoot this many times and still can't hit a dumb deer, they have no chance of hitting you!*

Now the cold was really getting to my feet. Part of the trouble was from the snow in my shoes, which accumulated during the walk from the motel to the car, but there was also the snow that piled into the sides of my shoes from the walk to the stand. This had increased the amount of water in my shoes. Added to this was the snow taking up space within my galoshes, which had turned to water and was evaporating into who-knows-where in this snowstorm. Unfortunately, this was adding to the cooling my feet felt. My pant legs were wet through two layers and the long john underwear beneath.

John had told me that these were good spots for the stands and that deer should walk by here real often. My only thought at this point was, *They better hurry by here so I can shoot one before I am either hit by a stray bullet, freeze into a statue on this stand, or slip on the slippery surface of the stand and fall to the ground.*

By this time, dawn had passed, and the light had become the light of a heavily overcast day. The snow had let up quite a bit but had not completely stopped. The visibility had become a lot better. Just so I would know, I began to look around and locate where the other hunters were positioned in the field behind me. I was able to identify the positions of five orange vests.

I'm not surrounded! The thought calmed my instant panic. *I can still retreat to the south toward the road!* What was I thinking? *We are supposed to all be on the same side, we hunters! The deer were the enemy.* Now, however, I became more apprehensive and began to look not only in front of me for the deer, but also to each side and to the rear.

The persistent shooting had only lasted a short time and had slowly come to an end. Things around me began to quiet down. I even began to lose some of the adrenaline rush I felt after the bullet whizzed by. Either I had pumped enough blood to my feet to have warmed the water in my shoes or my feet were frozen solid because they were no longer feeling so cold. The only time my legs felt the damp cold was when I moved them. I looked around at the fellow deer hunters and decided to wait a while longer for the elusive deer. Somehow, during this time, the warm glow returned as memories of Linda Leigh worked their way back into my mind.

It so happened, as it might with any ten-year-old boy, that Linda had somehow affected me, and I was having what might have been called at the time a "crush" on her. I really did not know her that well. I was attracted to her blond hair, cut somewhat short and curled in such a way to form a small wreath of hair all around the top of her head. The hair actually framed and accented her blue eyes and peaches-and-cream complexion. She was everything I had ever dreamed of seeing in a girl; she was Helen of Troy, Brunhilda, and the Virgin Mary all wrapped into one—although I don't remember ever seeing a picture of the Virgin Mary depicted with blond hair. I just could not build a pedestal high enough for her. She was all girlhood wrapped into that one person. This was my secret. I could never tell a soul. But I knew! And like all boys that age, I had to try my darndest to do things to get her attention.

I couldn't be overt about it. I couldn't do anything that would embarrass her. I had to be careful so I didn't become the one starting the fight by being accused of liking Linda. On the other hand, I could accuse someone up that pecking order of liking someone else. That would call attention for sure. It worked, but the attention obtained was from the teacher, and I got to know the other boy quite well as we copied dictionary pages together for many recess periods.

Well, dumb move; on to my next debacle. The one thing that trying to get her attention did for me was to start me off on a bad foot with the school administration. I was this outsider from Chicago and had already been marked as a troublemaker. In many respects, that became a self-fulfilling prophecy. Needless to say, I did get Linda's attention, but it didn't happen at school.

During the winter months, the YMCA had a program on Saturday mornings for the boys in town. It was a kind of basketball league called the Friendly Indians. Today, that would be a politically incorrect name, and something would have to be done about it, but then it was a good winter program for the city boys. I have no memory of how I became a member of that program or even much about it anymore. I was never very good at basketball anyway. In addition to that program was a program on Saturday afternoon at the local movie theater, the Rialto. The movies were specially picked for their appeal to the parents so the parents would send their children to these wholesome movies to keep them out of trouble.

The movies picked must have been popular with the parents, as the tickets for the seats at each showing were sold out for the year. It so happened that my mom thought it a good idea for me to play basketball with the Friendly Indians in the morning, get a hot dog at Fritzke's Cigar Shop—he had the best hot dogs in town, according to her—and then go to the movie. I was mostly a loner, not having penetrated the pecking order of the group of boys that were in my class, so I did all this by myself.

One Saturday, it was colder than usual, and I decided to get to the Rialto early. Being one of the first there, I picked a row halfway back from the screen and sat in the middle seat. This was my perfect seat from which to watch any movie. The theater seats filled up pretty fast, but the seats to my right in that row remained empty. There were too few seats in the row for most of the groups of kids that wanted to sit with each other. They went to areas where there were more open seats together. Finally, just before the feature began, Linda and her friends came and were ushered to these open seats. I couldn't believe it! There she was, the girl on my pedestal, with the only open seats left in the theater right beside me. She led her friends down the row and sat in the seat right beside me. If I had been a gentleman, I would have helped her remove her coat in such a cramped area, but I was in *like*, so the proper thing for a boy in *like* to do was to try to totally ignore her without letting on that you even cared.

Either it was obvious I wasn't caring or maybe I just looked natural because she said, "Hi."

Now this took *like* to a new height. I had to say something. I was scared, tongue-tied, and probably blushing in that dark theater, but did manage to whisper some coherent words back to her. We ended up watching the movie kind of together. We commented back and forth during the movie and even sat and talked about mundane things during the intermission when the rest of her friends went out to the front to buy candy. Finally, it was time to get up and leave. Before leaving, she whispered she would meet me again the same place next Saturday if I would like to. I indicated that I would be there and save the seats.

This friendship continued to build during the rest of the movie season. We never did anything to attract attention during the week, but at the Rialto on Saturday afternoon, we were best friends.

It was a common practice during those years that in the winter, when all the crops were sold and the next years farming was in the planning stage, farms would be bought and sold. Some of the farmers renting their farms would also move from one location to another. It was during this spring farming ritual when John Stemple turned up in the fourth grade at Edgerton public schools. His father had just bought a farm on one of the roads intersecting Highway 184 south of Fulton.

John had been going to school in Janesville, and his folks didn't want him attending one of the many small, one-room schools that were so common in the farming areas during those years. His father paid tuition for him to attend "town school." What was even more amazing was that his mom drove him to school each morning and then came and got him each afternoon. He would meet her at Ellingson's Hudson Garage across from the school playground. They drove Hudson cars. I guess that was a natural place to meet, and it was convenient. Sometime later, his Aunt Lorene moved to town, and he would sometimes go to her house after school.

John and I were in the same boat concerning the pecking order in class. He didn't fit either. That gave the two of us a common ground, and neither of us was the leader. We were equals and totally ignored the male hierarchy in the class. You hear stories about how Robin Hood and his best friend had to fight first before they could become best friends. That makes good drama for a story, but true friends don't necessarily have to meet that way.

We just got along together. It was natural. Later, we somehow attracted some of the lower end of the pecking order, and by the time spring rolled around, we had more guys in our "gang"—similar, but different meaning than today—than the class pecking order had. Yet we were different, and the two groups did different things.

"Hey up there! Are you frozen, dead, or just asleep?"

That call from behind and below my stand broke into my chain of memories. The snow had stopped, and what wind there was had died down. I wasn't feeling so cold, so the weather seemed milder than earlier.

"Just trying not to scare the deer away," I replied.

"I was just wondering," he responded. "The rest of us are going in. We usually do at 9:00 a.m. We come back out at about 3:00 p.m. and stay 'til dark. By the way, you must be the friend John Stemple said was coming to hunt with him."

I unloaded my shotgun and slowly began the slippery descent down the ladder from my perch. My feet were down there somewhere, but if I was blindfolded, I couldn't have told you where. I had to be very careful so they didn't slip off the rungs. My fingers weren't much better, but they finally wrapped around the ladder rungs enough so I didn't fall.

When I finally reached the ground, I formally introduced myself and explained John was off negotiating something or another and would be here as soon as possible. He introduced himself, but all I picked up was his last name: Riley. He said something about a Morrison and mentioned some other names I don't recall. He suggested I go to some store called Farm and Fleet in Janesville, try to look like a farmer, and get some "proper clothes before they'd have to drag my frozen carcass out of the field like a deer." I thanked him for his help and concern and said I would probably do that. His response was to the effect that because I was a rather big guy, Farm and Fleet would be the only place in Janesville that would have hunting clothes large enough for me on the shelf this late in the season.

His parting shot was, "This afternoon, I'll try not to shoot your way at any deer."

I began to limp my way across the field toward my Hertz rental Sable parked in the driveway to nowhere at the edge of Highway 59. As I approached the car, I considered the various ways I could get the car stuck in the mound of snow the county snowplough had so kindly left along the edge of the road behind the Sable. I needn't have worried. The snow was light, and as I backed out, it was easily pushed back by my car onto the road from where it had come. It did alert me, though, to make the observation that the snow was not melting. It was still crisp, light, and being occasionally blown in swirls by the slight wind.

Another portend of things to come was the heater in the rental car. As I retraced my route of the morning back to Janesville, the car couldn't begin to give heat until I reached Indian Ford.

After soaking in a tub of cold water to warm up and hanging my wet, half-frozen clothes over the shower curtain rod in the bathroom to dry, I dressed in some farmer clothes and went over to the Farm and Fleet store.

This store was really a great experience. It seemed to hold any kind of merchandise a farmer could want. Some of the things I saw in there brought back memories of the summers I worked with John at the Stemple farm. I found the clothing section, and Riley was right. I found thermal long underwear, thermal boots, thermal coveralls, thermal socks, and a proper orange hunting parka. *Boy,* I thought, *am I going to be a hit wearing this in Atlanta at the Charity Snowball Open Golf Tournament in a couple weeks! Not only will our foursome get the prize for worst score, but we may get the most outlandish costume prize, too.* I took all of the clothing to the cash register and found they even honored Visa cards there. The whole outfit came to just under $250, but at least I would be visible, waterproof, and warm this afternoon. I picked up a couple of Arby's roast beef sandwiches for lunch and went back to my room.

Back in the motel, I turned on the TV and caught about an hour of the Weather Channel. Good news for the deer; bad news for the hunters. A Canadian front was descending upon us, promising temperatures in the area of five degrees Fahrenheit. The snow had stopped for the time being, but it would be cold for about two days. The next pictures shown were of the high winds and drifting snow in Minneapolis and the cars denting each other as they slid to a stop on the icy streets.

I had expected the weather to be cold, but my memory of Thanksgiving holiday was one of being out in the field loading corn stalks onto a horse-drawn, flatbed wagon. There was a machine, a corn binder, I think it was called; it cut the cornstalks off at the ground and tied them into small bundles. The farmers would then stand the bundles up and lean them together to form the teepee-like structures called shocks. These structures stood in rows about ten feet from each other in the cornfield. The shocks would be left in the field until the farmer had time to bring them out of the field and into a barn. I can remember standing at the front of Stemple's wagon with the reins for driving the horses in my hands, trying to drive the team as John and Mr. Stemple loaded bundles of cornstalks onto the wagon from the corn shocks. Of course, we were never in any danger of my not driving the horses right because the horses listened to Mr. Stemple and not me, and they knew what to do in the field. When I was allowed to drive the wagon to the barn, the horses handled that easily too. They could find their way to the barn whether anyone was driving or not. I might have some vague memory of snow for Thanksgiving, but that snow was not deep enough to be memorable, and any details are lost. In any case, this was sure a change from the Atlanta weather I had left. And, to top it all off, the weather in Atlanta was going to be nice!

At about 2:30 in the afternoon, I began my drive through the peaceful countryside, blanketed in the cover of fresh snow. I turned into the driveway to nowhere and got out of the car. As I made my way to the stand through the snow, the only sounds I heard were from my new boots scrunching in the cold snow. I began to think, *If this silence keeps up, I will not know for the lack of shooting when the sun has officially set!*

I got back to my hunting spot and climbed back up on my stand. My only problem now was my hunting mittens; although they were warm, they were not made for a left-handed shooter. They were for a right-handed hunter. They had a little finger thing in the right-hand glove for the trigger finger. My trigger finger was in such a covering that I would have to remove the glove to shoot. I removed the mitten and loaded my gun. I easily got settled on my stand.

A while later, I noticed two deer come walking across the field from my left to my right. They came out of the brush at the far left side of the field, too far away for any of the hunters over by John's stand to have a good shot at them. From my vantage point, I couldn't determine if one or both were young bucks or a couple of doe. They were too far away to take any kind of a shot. Later still, I saw something gray come across the field in front of me. It looked like a small dog in pursuit of something running along on the ground in front of it. As it came closer, I recognized it as a gray fox in pursuit of a rather fast rabbit.

This afternoon was turning out a lot better than this morning. Although the air was colder, the snow had stopped falling, and my new clothes kept me very warm. The extra padding also made sitting that much easier. I looked around and spotted six hunters positioned around the fields behind me at critical junctures of woods and meadows. Any deer getting too close to any of them would be someone's dinner.

As I sat in the lonely stillness, my mind again began to drift to memories as warm to my mind as the warmth I felt sitting in my new, warm clothes. My thoughts jumped to my days in ninth grade. Linda was still my best friend. None of our parents would allow dating, so there were a bunch of us that chummed around together.

That fall, our bunch—I don't like to call it a gang, although that is what we called ourselves—went to all the high school home football games together. We would all buy our student tickets and meet in the stands, as those of us in freshmen class all sat in a section designated by the school administration. On many of those days, if John had been helpful around the farm, his dad would do all the chores himself and allow John to come to our house for supper before the game. We would then go together and meet the rest of the bunch at the game. Linda and I tried to sit near each other and yet not be an item. It seemed that we could always find some way, though, to just be special friends. John also had special friends, but they would change now and then, and you never knew who he was sitting near on any given week. Sometimes he would tell me; sometimes it would be a surprise.

Earlier, I referred to Linda as a soul mate, and I guess the easiest way to define the term is to say this was something that happened from fourth grade on and can best be described in this way. If I was going to a movie some night, which wasn't often, I would go alone. If I got there early, I would bump into her there with one of her friends, and we would sit together. I might go down to the Western Auto Store to get a bicycle part, and she would be there getting something for her dad, and we would talk for a while. Although we lived at different ends of town, we kept popping up at the same places together quite often without ever planning to do so. It happened so often that it became a habit of mine to look for her wherever I went because, generally, she would be there too.

So I guess it wasn't that out of the question that Linda and I would go to the game and to the dance after the game. Us guys were not much on dancing, but we went because the girl part of our gang did, and, somehow, where they went, we followed. The girls all had a great time dancing with each other while us guys would stand huddled together in one corner of the gym and rehash how we lost the game. This event happened most Friday nights all fall that year.

After football season was over, our gang had to look for places we could go together. One place was roller skating in Janesville. Later, we would meet to go ice-skating on the rink at Central Park. After Thanksgiving, the city would bank up the edges of the baseball field at the park and flood it. The water would freeze to a mirror surface, and this rink would be useable until early spring. Because in the summer the field was used for night softball games, it had large lights positioned in the outfield. These lights were used in the winter to give us evening skating.

John's mom turned out to be our driver. It was easier to fit all of us in the large front and back seats of that 1952 Hudson Hornet than in any of the other cars our parents owned. Also, it was during this time that Dad worked the late afternoon shift at the Fisher Body plant, which meant he took the family Chevy to work each night and I was without a parental ride. John's mom would bring John to town for these special occasions and go visit her sister while we did what we did. I will never forget that winter! I was young and somewhat shy, yet with the girl of my dreams. Each time we were together was fresh and exciting. After skating, we would go en-mass to someone's house for hot chocolate. John's mom would drive, and after the refreshments, she would drop us off one at a time at our respective homes. It was during these drives I began to feel sad and a little lonely when we dropped Linda at her house. I wished those nights would never end. Yet, we never talked of love. We never talked of going steady. Her pedestal was still high, and my self-confidence had not yet matured.

From my perch, I heard the report of a shotgun somewhat close behind me. I turned to see one of the orange-vested hunters walk out of the woods to my right and claim his deer. From my vantage point, it looked like he had shot a doe. If I had an in-state license, I too could have shot a doe, but my out-of-state license clearly stated I must shoot only a buck. After the kill, the rest of the men waiting in the field came out of their hiding places, walked over to the animal, and inspected the kill. Then the hunter who shot the animal began to field dress it.

Big light bulb! When I had asked John what I had to do if I shot a deer, he told me not to worry; he had field-dressed several and would show me how on the first one we shot. That answer suited me fine until now, when I realized if a deer went down by my slug, guess who would have to do the honors? I watched from the safe distance of my stand, not wanting to show my complete ignorance again today. I thought this morning's performance with the wet and frozen clothes had already placed the seed of laughter in the minds of the orange vests in the field behind me. They worked with the animal until someone pulled a small rope from his pocket. He tied it in such a way that two of them could drag the animal across the snow and out of the field. They probably had a vehicle close by to take the kill to be recorded.

I climbed down from my stand, as I guessed it was getting dark anyway and the day's hunt was probably at an end. As I was picking up the cartridges I dropped while unloading the gun before coming down from the stand, Riley came up to the fence again.

"You looked a lot healthier in those warm clothes this afternoon," he said.

"I feel a lot warmer for sure," I replied.

"John gonna be hunting tomorrow with you?" Riley asked.

"I sure wish he could," I replied. "But he said he would be here by Thanksgiving Day at the latest."

"You gonna be out here for sunrise tomorrow morning?" questioned Riley.

"You bet," I replied as enthusiastically as I could.

I didn't want them to think this city guy was the least bit daunted by this experience. It is always best to put on a good front for the natives. I figured they would have plenty to laugh about tonight anyway when my hunting was brought up.

When I returned to the motel room, I found my message light was on. I sat on the edge of the bed, called the desk, and was told to call John's wife. They gave me a number. When I called her, she told me the material John was trying to buy from the supplier didn't check out and that he was going to have to go to Mexico next week to fill the needs. John would not be able to arrive until next Saturday at the earliest, and he would probably fly into Chicago and need to be picked up. She added one piece of helpful advice. Since the deer were so plentiful and I was sure to get one, she suggested that I go to the Edgerton public library. She thought I probably remembered where it was. She suggested I find a book about deer hunting and xerox the pages showing how to field dress a deer so I didn't look too much like city slicker.

Great thought! Next time I talk with her, I want to find out why she chose to stay home from this hunting trip anyway. She would have been a great help.

I was tired, so I went out of the motel to forage for food. I found a Mexican restaurant at the edge of the shopping mall on Highway 14 where I ate a good meal. I watched a little TV and went to bed.

The Cold Sets In

It is Sunday night, and the big news is I hunted twice again today, the same as yesterday. I decided getting up at 4:30 was for the birds. I couldn't hunt until 6:30 anyway, so why get there so early? In any case, sitting out there in zero-degree weather would be no picnic. I got up at 5:30 instead, dressed quickly in my new clothes, stopped at the quick stop, and was still at my stand by 6:30. The temperature announced on the Madison radio station was minus five degrees Fahrenheit with a five-to-ten-mile north wind. The temperature announced in Janesville was zero degrees with a ten-to-fifteen-mile-an-hour wind from the north, northwest. From that information, I guessed the temperature at the stand had to be below zero; I didn't even guess about the wind.

The car barely got warm before I reached my parking place. The walk to the stand convinced me that sitting up there in cold and the wind was not going to be the smartest thing I had ever done. I decided I would show myself at the stand, wave to Riley and the boys, and then kinda stand in the weeds along the fencerow. I concluded any deer that couldn't see a bright orange-vested man must be pretty blind, which led me to conclude that until it got warmer, the deer would have to tolerate my not playing by their rules.

One advantage I found in standing was that I could position myself better against the wind and shield my face better from the cold. The other thing I found, though, was my nose was not acclimated to the cold anymore, and the glasses I was wearing became very cold and made matters worse. As it got lighter, I looked around and could see more. Nothing was stirring. The deer must be bedded down somewhere, as any self respecting animal should know better than to come out in weather this cold.

As before, when I found the hunt to go slow, I began to think back to that year when I was a freshman in Edgerton High School. I thought about Linda and that spring.

I was an adventuresome youth. I didn't steal or use a lot of bad language, but I was excited by speed and feats of daring. I desperately wanted a motorcycle. Being a James Dean fan, I wanted to wear my hair in what was at the time known as a DA cut. I wanted a black leather jacket and stomping boots. As you might suspect, my parents wanted nothing to do with my interest in this alternate lifestyle. I wanted to save up for a leather jacket. Mom was sympathetic. Dad was outright against it. This little problem persisted. Dad took me down to the sheriff's office in Janesville and showed me pictures of motorcycle accidents where the riders had either been killed outright or badly mangled. At school, the people riding motorcycles were jokingly referred to as temporary Americans. But youth will be youth, and youth loves excitement. I even thought the more dangerous the activity that created the excitement, the more alluring the activity was. In looking back, I believe I could call it "the moth and the candle flame" syndrome.

There was another part that played a role in this, and that was how impressive the act might be to the girl one wanted to impress. The secret to impressing girls, though, is to do something that appears to be very dangerous but, in fact, has been rendered safe. I believe I learned that one a little too late though.

One afternoon in late April, a number of us were standing around after school outside Jake Disrud's malt shop. Linda was there, along with a number of my other school friends. This fellow drives up with this super-looking Harley. He was an upperclassman and was showing off his newly paid-for bike. He was a little cocky and was offering to take some of the girls for rides. He had it all: speed, excitement, and a way to impress the girls with the danger. None of the girls would go for a ride with him. Then he asked the older guys. Most brushed him off and declined, some commenting that it was too dangerous.

The desire to impress Linda took hold of me. This was the ultimate: my dream of impressing her by doing something involving speed, excitement and danger. I said something to Linda, got on the back of the bike, and said loud enough for all to hear the challenge above all challenges, "Show me what this thing can do!"

The cyclist was wearing riding clothes: leather jacket, tight pants, and leather boots. I was wearing loose, cotton slacks with one-inch, cuffed leg bottoms; oxford shoes with cotton socks; and a cotton coat with large side pockets.

I sat behind him, and we roared up and down Swift Street with him showing me what the bike could do in the length of that one city block. It was fun, it was exciting, and it looked dangerous. I was thrilled!

What caused the accident was the sand on the road at the end of the block, spread there on the ice before it melted. We had an audience, and they were all watching when, in a quick, end-of-the-block turn to the right at West Fulton Street, the bike hit the sand and dumped.

When it went over, he got clear. The cuff on my loose trousers got caught on some part of the cycle, pulling my right leg under the cycle when it dumped. The hose fitting for the hose from the gas tank to the carburetor broke off, spraying gas at my crotch and down my right leg. My cotton coat and my right pants leg became wet with gasoline. The weight of the cycle on the tibia of my right leg broke it, and the bone sticking out of the leg began to be ground away on the pavement. As the cycle and I slid along on the pavement, the friction and the sparks from the steel abrading on the cement of the street caught the gasoline on the ground on fire. It didn't take long until the gasoline on my clothing caught fire.

At that moment, I could just envision the picture of my charred body next to the wrecked bike on the wall display board at the sheriff's office in Janesville. As the fire got hotter and the flames got closer to my face,

I watched in slow motion horror as the bike finally came to a halt in the middle of West Fulton Street.

The next thing I remember is being in a hospital. I don't even now know where they took me. I vaguely remember Vaseline being rubbed on me and getting shots of something, but for a while, my memory never was clearer than just a blur. Because of my broken tibia, I eventually ended up in the orthopedic ward at the University of Wisconsin hospital in Madison.

My recovery was slow and painful. There were skin grafts. There was the short right leg. There was nerve damage to my back and all of the other things that had to be overcome. I was tutored so I didn't lose my grade in school, and I finally returned to Edgerton High School in the middle of my junior year.

The only person who kept in touch with me throughout the whole ordeal was John. I asked about Linda from time to time, but he always avoided giving an answer.

Back in school, I was still using crutches while my right leg strengthened. I walked with a limp but tried to hide the lift on the now-shorter leg as best I could. I tried to look as normal as possible. I worked hard at walking, so the limp caused by my shorter right leg didn't show. I don't think I ever really was able to cover the limp. Even now, it is still with me. The kids I had chummed around with all had changed. The old gang was gone. I hadn't seen Linda. I wasn't in any of her classes. In the hospital, I had begun pursuing classes that would lead me into an engineering college, so it was natural that I took the math and sciences offered. Because of the times they were scheduled, I ended up on a different class schedule than the kids I formerly hung around with. Because of this, I ended up in the class schedule with the farm kids.

After about a month of attending classes, and after discarding my crutch, one day I chanced to meet Linda accidentally in a hall after school. I was on the way to meet with a teacher, and she was coming from a class activity. She seemed to want to avoid stopping and talking. There was no graceful way she could, so she stopped. I don't remember the exact dialogue, but the gist of it was that a girl had to look out for her future, and she had no confidence that I could ever provide her with the kind of life she wanted.

I was jogged back to reality. As I looked around, it seemed as though everyone else had left the field, so I unloaded the gun, headed back to the Sable, and drove to Janesville to eat a Sunday brunch. I also wanted to relax before returning later in the afternoon to watch for some action from the deer.

When I returned to the motel, the desk clerk asked me how the hunt was going. I told him nothing had happened yet. We laughed. After changing clothes, I stopped off at a cafeteria in a shopping center in Janesville and had a light lunch. After lunch, I decided the best way to relax would be by driving around Janesville to see what landmarks I remembered.

The sheriff's office had been moved. It was now out on the Highway 14 bypass on the property I remembered as the county farm and old folk's home. I remember it also being referred to as the "poor farm." This was the place where the indigent were supposedly housed and detained during the depression. It was always held up to the children as the place they would go if they did not do certain things, as in, "If you don't study hard, you will end up at the poor farm." I wondered if the sheriff still had a wall covered with pictures of motorcycle accidents. Better yet, I wondered if the pictures of me ever made that wall.

Driving into the city on Business 51, I passed the new (in the fifties) Parker Pen Factory. I wondered if the current owners of the Parker Pen name even use that plant anymore. I found a new bridge across the Rock River that led to the hospital and Riverside Park. Because of the snow and all, I didn't venture down into Riverside Park, but I remembered the exciting times I had in the summer when Mom and Dad would take me for a picnic to Riverside Park.

It would usually end with me begging for a Sunday afternoon ride on the *Silver Queen* boat. I believe the rides stopped, and the boat disappeared long before my folks left Edgerton.

The *Silver Queen* was an excursion boat that would shove off from a concession stand/pier and move leisurely upstream for a Sunday cruise on the Rock River. The boat had to be at least fifty feet long and twenty feet wide. The bow reminded me of a shrunken Great Lakes ore boat, while the second half was an open deck comprised of a dance floor with chairs pushed against the railing all the way around the deck. In the bow section, there was a phonograph that played the popular dance songs of the day. More prominent, though, was the concession stand.

Under the dance floor was an engine room. One time, when the doors were opened on the dance floor, I looked down into the engine room and found it cramped, to say the least. As far as I know now, this could have been nothing more than a gussied up barge with an engine placed in it. No mater what it actually was, to me, it was the most beautiful and fascinating boat I had ever seen. It is long gone, but the memory, for a moment, lingered on.

Following the road that seemed to have been City 14, I passed Janesville's direct connection with important history. When I was growing up, it was called the Tallman House. Now it is called the Tallman Restoration. The house itself is yellow brick, basically square, two stories high, with a hip roof topped by a four-sided room-like cupola at the apex. The cupola had windows on four sides and reminded me of the top of a lighthouse.

The history claimed by the house concerned the night Abraham Lincoln was said to have slept in the bed in one of the rooms. There were those who never believed it, but because of it, the house was open for tours. As I got older, I learned more about the house. It, being on a sandstone bluff along the Rock River, was in an excellent position to have a secret river level opening to a tunnel leading up to the house. This made it possible for persons to be secretly brought to the house and taken away. Some supposedly secret rooms were found, and the inference was that the house was a stop in the Underground Railroad before the Civil War. That bit of historical speculation had the historical society buzzing for quite some time. I remember Dad coming home from the Chevy plant and telling Mom and me some of the stories connected with that house.

I drove past the house and continued out of Janesville until Business 14 intersected Highway 14. I then headed back to my motel room to dress for the hunt.

On my way to the field, I decided it would be worthwhile to drive through Edgerton for the first time in forty years. Until now, I had been too distracted by the snow, the cold, and the hunt to do this. I also thought I should take a look at the old library to make sure it was where I had last left it.

As I remembered Edgerton, the south side began at the bluff overlooking the Rock River. Highway 51 is a north-south highway bisecting the city. As you enter from the south and cross the Rock River, the land to the north rises somewhat to form a small ridge that drops off a little where South Main Street begins. That small ridge continues to the right about two blocks and turns to the parallel Highway 51. As you drive north on Highway 51, past the center of town, the ridge drops off for Saunders Creek to pass through it. Over that ridge to the east are a little valley with Saunders Creek at the bottom and then another large hill. East-west Highway 59 bisects the town and travels east and west through it. If you turned right on Highway 59 and drove over that ridge, you would drive down the hill into the small valley, cross the bridge over Saunders Creek, and drive up one of the steepest hills in the town. I believe it was called New York Hill, but I have no idea why. If you turn west, the land is flat until you proceed out of town, where it rises slightly. The city nestles in what could be considered a kind of bowl. In the southwest quadrant is an area that was considered lowland by some and a swamp by others. The land at the crossing of Highways 51 and 59, though, was pretty level, and that part of the town was on what I would call the flat, which was somewhat higher than the lowland, but more or less in the center of the bowl. Farther to the north and curving around to the west were ridges from several small hills. On the other hand, compared to Lilburn, Georgia, Edgerton is flat!

I drove into town from the south on Highway 51, Main Street, and turned left on Highway 59, West Fulton Street. I drove on West Fulton about two and one-half city blocks and turned right on Albion Street, which intersects West Fulton at an angle.

I drove past a few houses and came to the building I remembered. The architecture of the Edgerton Library can best be described as Greek revival done on a limited budget. It has columns, a Greek-type façade, and is built with a rectangular floor plan. The brick is the color of dark sandstone and, in the late forties, seemed to match the perception we, as students, had of what an ancient Greek temple of learning should look like.

I drove to Rollins Street, made a right-hand turn, and followed it to Swift Street. I turned right at the stop sign at Swift. I now was on the street where the accident had happened. When I was young, the buildings on my left were the grade-school buildings, and the ones on my right were the Catholic church; the rectory; the high school classroom building; and, next to it, the gym. Continuing along on the right was the post office building and the Pontiac dealership; on my left, the fourth through eighth-grade school building, the first- and second-grade school building, several houses, the blacksmith shop, Jake Disrud's malt shop, and some other buildings.

Progress has taken that part of town and stripped it of the scholastic glamour it had in my youth. The gym is now a senior citizens' center. All of the old school buildings have been preserved and redone as senior citizens' apartments. It seems ironic that some of the same people who spent their early years in school at that location are now spending their last days there in the retirement community. The post office still functions. I have no idea what is now in the building that housed the Pontiac garage. The blacksmith shop is now a drive-through car wash, and Jake Disrud's malt shop houses a craft shop.

I turned west on Highway 59 and drove to my stand to begin the cold afternoon hunt. I was there at 3:00 p.m. I braved the cold breeze bundled up in my warm hunting clothes. I got settled on my stand by 3:15. The orange vests arrived a little later. I wondered what was keeping them. I mused they probably fell upon a doe by accident on their way in and, having scared it to death, had to remove it from the field and report it in to the county inspectors. Taking the carcass to have it legally inspected was something I was reading about from the Wisconsin hunters' rulebook last night.

The field-dressed carcass had to be transported so it could be seen by anyone who looked at the vehicle to which it was tied. I was wondering how the Hertz counter people would react if I brought the Sable back with bloodstains on the paint across the trunk. I have heard that sometimes bloodstains are almost impossible to remove from automotive paint. This trip might be even more costly than I originally thought! I began to devise ways that I could place the deer carcass on the back of the Sable without rope and without spoiling the paint. I had neither rope to tie it on with nor plastic to protect the paint.

I looked down and saw, not thirty feet away, what looked to be a medium-sized deer, pawing away snow and eating some of the grass it uncovered. I couldn't see the head well enough to determine if the deer was a buck or a doe. I quietly removed the glove from my left hand and let it drop to the ground. The deer had not heard the slight noise. I brought the gun to my shoulder and was able to release the safety without the deer noticing this either. I was ready to pull the trigger when the deer turned its head and I could get a good heart shot. The darn thing moved so the tail was closer to me. From the angle I was at, I could not determine for sure it was a buck. I could get a perfect rump shot, which would not bring him down. I waited, trying not to move. The gun was becoming heavier by the moment. Slowly, I tried to move to place my foot at the edge of the ladder to the stand to steady my leg so I could lean the shotgun on it. Still, the deer didn't notice. *A really deaf deer must have wandered into my sights,* I thought. *This waiting can be tedious, but I can eat a small buck just as easily as a large one. Come on, deer. Turn around! I want to see the size of that rack.* I don't know how long that deer was grazing, but my arms were so tired from holding the gun I almost put it down. My bare hand was beginning to really feel the cold. Not only was the back of the hand freezing from the below-freezing temperature, but the inside of my hand was having the heat drained from it by the below-freezing temperature of the metal shotgun it was gripping so tightly. At least I found my deer.

Now this is the excitement of the hunt! You spot the deer, your adrenaline surge happens, and then you sit and freeze to death waiting for the stupid animal to turn so you can take a good shot. After what had to have been about a half hour, the deer, with his hind quarters to me and with his head low, began to walk slowly to the south, getting farther and farther away from me. If I had a doe tag, I would have wounded him in the rump and got him with a second shot. As it was, I think he was a buck, but at that distance, without binoculars, I was unable from the rear to make out enough detail of his anatomy, and so he walked away.

At least I saw a deer! I tried to push the safety on the gun with my frozen hand but had trouble. I gingerly took off the other glove and pushed it to the safety position. I unloaded the gun. *Now to warm up my exposed hand*, I thought. I didn't remember what frostbite looks like, but this was the first time I ever did such a dumb fool thing to my hand anyhow. Well, the sun looked like it had dropped low in the sky. The orange vests were still in the field, but I thought I had seen my deer for the day. I came down from my stand, picked up my glove, and walked back to the car to warm my hands.

Back at the motel, I took stock of my situation. I needed to make another run to Farm and Fleet for supplies. I needed rope, plastic, something to protect my nose, a pocket watch, and better hunting gloves. I also wondered if they had medical supplies, as my hand burned as though it had been held in a fire for too long a time. The hand looked red and sore, but that is the price one has to pay for a deer that would not move.

As I walked through the motel lobby, the clerk asked how the hunt today had gone. I told him about the deer and how uncooperative it had been. We discussed the correct stalking procedure, and he offered some advice. It included things like looking the deer in the eye, not shooting until you see the blue of the eyes, and talking to them in Norwegian. He claimed one can lure them closer to the stand if you talk Norwegian to them. After all this good advice, I concluded that he was rooting for the deer. He also said that you can tell the sex of the deer by looking at the tail. That seemed fairly obvious. This comment included something about there being white under the tail of a doe.

As I finished cleaning up and got ready to go out to eat, it occurred to me to make a list of all the things I would have to do tomorrow to have all my bases covered. First, I would have to go to the stand at sunrise. I would have to visit the Farm and Fleet store at 10:00 a.m. when it opened. By 11:30, I should be at the Edgerton Public Library obtaining information on field dressing a deer. While there, I probably should look up references to talking Norwegian to the deer—haha. I would definitely follow up on white tails on deer. I would have to be back at the motel by 2:00 p.m. to dress for the hunt. This looked to be a lot of activity for the day, but if I stuck to the plan, it should work.

After changing clothes, I went to the Sable and drove around looking for a restaurant that looked inviting. For some reason, eating alone doesn't appeal to the traveling salesman. On the other hand, one must be careful to pick the right kind of restaurant or eating can become even lonelier. This is particularly true when families are present in the place where one is eating. When I was younger, bars and clubs held a great allure, but you get sick and tired of them also. Tonight, I couldn't find a place that appealed to me in my current frame of mind. I finally settled for a coke and an Arby's roast beef. I took these back to my room and ate in front of the TV. There was nothing memorable on the tube either.

The Lady in the Library

It is Monday night, and I have had a most interesting day. Let me tell you again about surprises; today has been full of them. The day started out with an early morning phone call from John Stemple; the first surprise. He apologized for the problem he was having, but he would have to spend the whole week in Mexico. He wouldn't even make it back for the weekend! If the materials he was procuring were sufficiently stockpiled at the plant, he could wait on this, but if he doesn't find material soon, there will be layoffs at the plant. We discussed the deer population, the temperature outdoors, and the orange vests to the north of me. I assured him I was okay and hadn't shot an orange-vested deer yet. He told me to keep it that way. We said good-bye and hung up.

It was cold again this morning. The official temperature was near five degrees below zero. I went through the dress-for-the-hunt ritual and left the motel to go to the stand. I parked the car and began the walk across the field against a rather stiff wind. It was coming from the northwest and must have been about 8 mph, with gusts to 20 mph. My new clothes were warm, but my glasses frames were becoming very cold. I had to hold my glove in front of my face to protect the nose sticking out there and to keep the gusts of wind from taking my breath away. The snow was crisp, and when I stepped into the footprints I had made the previous day, the snow gave off a crunchy sound. I had to stop often just to get my breath!

I didn't expect to see many deer on a day like this. I guessed they would all be bedded down for the day someplace sheltered and out of the wind.

When I reached my stand, I decided to climb up and look around. This was the first morning the sky was cloudless. There above me was a full moon shining down on the white snow blanket. From the top of the stand, I could see all around. When I looked north, I saw no orange vests. The time was nearing sunrise, and the woods were empty of hunters. I looked around and thought I saw something brown move. Could I be seeing deer moving this early in the morning? I finally concluded that it must be a mirage or an optical illusion caused by the wind.

I decided to sit on the platform for a little while. I am a large person; I would consider myself bulky, but not bulky enough to become a sail. As I was perched on top of the stand, a forceful gust of wind hit my back and seemed to push the stand a little away from the tree it leaned against. I moved my weight back and finally it settled back tight against the tree again. Those were some pretty strong gusts, and they unnerved me. I decided I would do as the deer and make myself a little nest in the weeds beneath the stand for protection against the wind.

I unloaded my shotgun and climbed down from the stand. I chose a spot right beneath the stand and started to clear the snow from the weeds and grass I found there. Soon, I had a nice, round area about three feet in diameter cleared of almost all the snow that had drifted there. In the cleared area, the brown grass made a soft-looking bed on which to sit. I had bent the taller weeds to the sides to get them out of the way. Finally, I centered myself in the cleared circle and crouched down to wait the appearance of the deer. Sitting low in the grass and weeds, my imagination ran wild, and I thought, *This must be like it would be if I was in a duck blind or maybe some protected shelter. I could see how if the deer settled in like this the cold weather might not be too uncomfortable for them.*

Originally, I was worried about crouching down like that in case one of the orange vests would mistake me for a deer and I would get shot. I still didn't see any orange vests, so I felt safe to sit mostly concealed in this nest. I found my little nest protected me from most of the wind. The dried grass seemed to insulate me from the cold ground, and I became comfortable. I didn't think many deer would be on the move, so I was vigilant over a very narrow area. This gave me the opportunity to again remember and dream.

I remembered back to the spring of my junior high school year. Dad came home one evening and announced his promotion up the ranks at GM. He was to go to Detroit and work in one of the divisions at the corporate engineering level. He would leave in May, and Mom and I would follow after school was out. He would find a place to live and prepare it for our arrival. These things happen. People move all of the time. The people in the military are more affected by this than others, but they are not unique. John Stemple was the only true friend I had left after all the time I was away. I was no longer close with any of the others in my class. They wouldn't miss me, and, in reality, they had changed. I no longer even knew them.

When school was out, Mom and I left, following the moving truck. With the new job, Dad got a classy-looking 1957 Chevy with a V8 engine. Because of the accident, I didn't have the time yet to get my driver's license, so Mom did the driving. I navigated for her. That was the easy part, keeping my eyes on the back of the moving van. Mom had the hard part; she had to drive fast enough to keep the van in sight. That became tricky as we worked our way through the Chicago traffic; the Gary traffic; the little town traffic; and, finally, the Detroit area traffic.

Dad bought a beautiful older house in Royal Oak. We moved in and found that even the carpets and furniture fit. I spent the summer growing stronger and trying to forget the sad experiences I had in Edgerton. John and I wrote back and forth for about a year but finally, as things happen, he and I each were sidetracked by what was happening around us. I never heard from any of my other classmates.

As I was musing over the ways in which we lose track of old friends, I noticed a large buck coming toward me from over the knoll to the southwest. The wind was blowing from the northwest, and he had not caught my scent yet. As he got closer, he was not just a buck. This had to be the stag in this area. I believe he fit the definition of a stag. His rack was enormous. His bearing was regal, as he slowly walked along, angling toward me. He was at least one hundred yards away and looked as though that would be as close as he would get if he kept his current course. I had a big problem. I wanted to shoot him, but using a shotgun slug at that distance was about as effective as throwing rocks, so I never even took the gun off safety. As I watched him walk away, the thought came into my mind that what was needed to hunt here was a shotgun with a rifled barrel and a scope attached to that barrel. Then at least the hunter would have a chance.

I peeled back some layers of clothing and looked at my watch. It read 9:30! Already, I was half an hour late. If I wanted to get on schedule to do what I had to today, I had better hurry. I packed everything up and headed to Janesville.

I got to the Farm and Fleet store fifteen minutes late, according to my schedule. I bought a plastic tarp, some rope, a pocket watch, better gloves, salve for my frostbitten hand, a nose protector, and a knife for gutting the deer. I was more efficient than I had been previously and was checked out by 11:00. I drove directly to the Edgerton Public Library and was there right on schedule.

I went to the desk and got the attention of the librarian. I interrupted what she was doing to ask her where to look to find information on gutting a deer and how I would be able to Xerox the information. She was very helpful and immediately called to her assistant, asking her to help me find what I was looking for.

I didn't immediately see the face of the assistant, as her head was bent down to look at something on the table where she was working. There was something vaguely familiar about her voice, though, as she asked what specifically I wanted.

The librarian did not introduce me by name; she only asked this mysterious lady, "Could you interrupt what you are doing and help this man find some information?"

"What I need is a book that shows how to gut a deer so I can get a Xerox copy to take with me while I am hunting here," I stated.

She looked up abruptly from what she was doing as though someone had shocked her and asked, "What is your name?"

"Peter Waldmann. Why do you ask?"

At that, she slowly, as though in shock, sat down in the chair behind the table, and I got a chance to look into that face. Her hair was mostly gray, with just a hint of blond left in it. It was permed in a style that formed a silver halo, framing her face. The face looked fatter or maybe a little puffier than I remembered, but it was definitely the face that went with the voice. I suddenly attached to a name from the depths of my memory.

"You are Linda Swensen, aren't you?" I asked.

"I was Linda Swensen," she answered, "but for the last thirty-two years, it has been Linda Sandersen."

My immediate desire to Xerox anything about a deer just took a backseat to the realization that some part of her pedestal was still there. Suddenly, I felt the beginning of a lump growing in my throat. For a few moments, I was without words, which is a very unnerving thing when you are a salesman and live by your words.

Finally, I was able to respond with the first thing that came to mind. "Strange weather we are having this early in the year."

That inane comment apparently broke the ice, as she looked up at me with a quizzical look on her face and we both began to laugh.

"What have you been doing with yourself these last twenty or thirty years?" she asked.

"Selling Capital Equipment to the textile, chemical, and pulp/paper industries," I answered. "What have you been doing?"

There was a long pause, and then she asked, "Do you have a family?"

Changing the subject like that kind of telegraphed a problem to me, a seller of equipment. She either was acting coy, or there were problems with Mr. Sanderson. Either way, she did not want to commit information to me until she knew more about my situation. I had to think long and hard to be able to even consider how to truthfully answer that question.

"Both my parents are dead; I was an only child, so, in that sense, I don't have a family."

"I don't see a ring on the fourth finger of your left hand. Aren't you married?" she asked.

"That is a long story we don't have time for here," I answered. "What brought you to Wisconsin?"

"John Stemple and I were going to spend nine days hunting deer out west of town, but John had work that had to be done out of the country and had to back out. I guess you can say I came alone. That is why I need the information I asked for. As you might guess, I am not an experienced deer hunter."

"Where are you staying? John's folks died long ago, and the Sayres bought the farm, so I know you are not staying there," she replied.

"I have a room at the Holiday Inn Express on the Highway 14 bypass in Janesville," I replied.

"It would be nice to get together and talk over old times while you are so close."

"I could meet you and your husband some evening this week, as I have very little to do after sunset and the nights are getting longer every day," I responded.

"It would have to be just the two of us; Mark and our three sons are up near Tomahawk hunting for deer with what they call 'real guns.' They plan to be there until Sunday," she said.

"Have they shot anything yet?"

"Not as of last night. They are hunting in woods and haven't even seen a deer yet."

"I have seen several so far. That is why I am here. If I shoot one, I have to find out what to do with it. When John and I planned this trip, he said it would be a new experience for me and he would show me how to gut the deer and all of that. Now that he will not be here, I need to find a book to tell me how to do it."

With a flourish, Linda got up out of her chair and led the way to an area of the stacks that contained books on butchering various animals. There, she found a book on deer processing that included everything from field dressing to salvaging the best cuts. I began to page through the book, looking for what I wanted to Xerox.

"Where do you live?" she asked.

"In Lithonia, Georgia; Atlanta is our largest suburb," I replied. That statement answers a lot of questions and puts things in perspective. It even gets a chuckle from some people. Linda laughed.

I didn't want to sound stupid, so I, a salesman of many words, tried to buy time by appearing to read areas in the book she had found for me. Deep inside, however, I felt this great confusion. Here was the woman on the pedestal where I had placed her so many years ago, the one who had been in the back of my mind hidden away and, even in fantasy, worshipped. The emotional hit from this was a hard one to control.

Here in front of me, married with three sons, was she, my friend whom so long ago rejected me; I, though rejected, had never given up my memory of her. How does one talk to this person and not seem foolish, not embarrass himself, not say something stupid, and not let his inner emotions show? I really had to come up with something to say as we worked together to find me the information I needed. Her helping me was a legitimate thing. It was the small talk while we worked together that was tying me up in knots.

I had asked her and her husband to meet me for dinner. Her husband was off deer hunting for the whole week. That was her answer. *Now is that the end of the conversation, or would it be proper for me to ask her if she would like to go to lunch with me? Or does she expect me to make a move in that direction? Or would she be offended if I should ask her? Yet, she brought it up first, and why this thing about food? Salesmen are notorious for feeding people. I guess that, by habit, they feel more comfortable conducting business over food. Yet, romance is also waged over food, albeit usually by candlelight in an evening setting.*

Here I am thinking about another man's wife! I never do this. Are my thoughts pure, as in friendship and old times, or are there other motives, more sinister? Am I too ashamed of myself for thinking about another man's wife that I can't even admit these thoughts to myself?

As I looked through the book, trying to appear as though I were reading, these concerns were hammering their way through my brain. I had to do something or say something, as she had moved so she was close to but a little behind me, looking over my left arm at the pages in the book I was appearing to read. Her perfume was distracting me even more as I felt the weight of her breath against the sleeve of my shirt. I turned back a few pages.

"Can we Xerox from page twenty-three to page twenty-nine?" I asked.

She took the book from me, and I followed her to the workroom where the machine was. From where I was standing, I was able to look at this woman and compare her with the vision from the forty-year-old memory I had stored in my mind. She was still nearly five feet six inches tall. Her hair was now more gray than blonde. Her eyes were still that special blue. Her figure showed the signs of having passed through menopause; her shoulders more rounded, her body more filled out and broadened, having been sacrificed to the three children she had borne. Her hands showed the signs of the physical abuse of one who found it necessary to do menial work. Yet, her step was still light, and there was that special lilt in her voice that had not gone away with age. Her face still held that special smile. The Virgin Mary she was not; Helen of Troy, well, maybe; but she still fit that image of Brunhilda I carried in my mind.

"Here are the copies you wanted," she said as she handed them to me.

"How much do I owe you?" I asked, remembering the sign noting a charge of twenty cents a copy.

"No charge; special friends get special privileges," she said as she gave me the current version of a smile I remembered from so long ago.

Before I had a chance to respond—I still didn't want to say something foolish—she said, "I'll call you at 7:00 tonight, so be in your room."

"I'll be there," I answered as I turned to leave.

"You better take the papers you came for," she said, giggling as she handed them to me.

I felt myself turning at least three shades of red in quick succession as I took the papers from her hand and silently exited, taking pains to open the door ahead of myself and watch my feet so as not to fall and embarrass myself further. I thought I was handling myself really good until the grand exit!

Here I am, this competent salesman who never leaves his briefcase in a buyers office by mistake, never misses an airplane flight, is always on time, always on top of the sale, and never flustered. What do I do but get so flustered by this woman I forget what I came for. What on earth will she think of me? Have my feelings been unmasked?

I got back in the Sable and began to turn around to go back to the motel to dress for the hunt when I got the urge to just keep driving up Albion Street to Washington Street. I had to drive by the old house just once. I had told myself when I planned this trip I would stay away from all those old scars and memories and not let the pain and regrets get to me. But now, after the library, the good memories had taken sway over the pain, although the regrets were still there.

As I turned from Albion left onto Washington, I almost got cold feet, wanting to turn left again on North 1st, but I forced myself to continue on and then to look at the house. John was right when he had said nothing changed in the forty years since I left. The house was the same and still the same color. The trees were old when I was there, and they seemed to not have changed. With the layer of snow on everything, it looked just like it did the last Christmas I had lived there. That bittersweet memory returned, of pain and accomplishment, anticipation, letdown, and social defeat. I came to Stoughton Road and turned left, heading back to West Fulton Street and the roads back to my motel.

I got back to my stand at about 3:30 this afternoon. After the library, the last thing I wanted to see was another deer. The weather had warmed some, and the sun had changed the consistency of the snow on the ground. It was more compactable than earlier, but had still resisted the melting process. I found the orange vests situated in the usual places, so I climbed to the top of my stand and made sure I was visible. *Getting shot by mistake still holds no appeal, but it probably isn't any worse than being embarrassed at a library!*

Linda Says it All

I began my vigil on my perch in earnest, trying to be the best deer hunter I possibly could. After the afternoon debacle at the library (the second surprise of the day), the very thought of Linda brought a flush of embarrassment, humiliation, and guilt. I might have let my emotions show through to a woman who had no business knowing what I felt. Besides, I skipped lunch, and the acids in my stomach were trying to eat their way out. The acid happens only when I am extremely upset.

Coming "home" brought other memories; not of Edgerton, but of Milwaukee and the woman I married. She was another ghost from the past better left to sleep, but seeing Linda upset the whole barrel of worms that, at this point, were all trying to wiggle around through my brain at the same time.

Her name was Jennifer Elaine Wilke. She was a native of the greater Milwaukee area. We met while I was a student at Milwaukee School of Engineering. To make sense of this, I must back up to just before Milwaukee.

I spent the year after graduating from high school in various hospitals to clean up the last of the obvious scar tissue from the accident. The doctors and nurses did their best, and my right arm and the outer portions of the right leg had come along rather nicely. They looked almost normal. The inside of my right leg up to my waist was another story.

By this time, John had left the farm and was attending a college somewhere out West. There was no one else in Edgerton I corresponded with, so I had no ties there.

My father, being an engineer at GM, found a way I could work my way through college. This was a time before society deemed it necessary for parents to pay their children's way through school, but a time when a good word from a relative of good repute could still pull some strings. My father, being in the GM system, knew about a GM study program for which I might qualify. There was this GM plant in Milwaukee called AC Spark Plug that had a work-study program in conjunction with Milwaukee School of Engineering (M.S.O.E.). All I had to do was qualify and I could get into the program.

The work-study program was keyed to the M.S.O.E. quarter system. You studied for two quarters and worked for two quarters. The shortest time a person could take to get an engineering degree from M.S.O.E. was thirty-six months full-time. The average academic load was nineteen to twenty-two quarter hours per quarter. It took eight years to get the engineering degree on the co-op program with AC Spark Plug. That meant for eight years I would live and work in Milwaukee. This was acceptable to me. The program worked out fine.

By this time, you are probably wondering where Jennifer fit into all of this. Due to the scarring and other problems brought about by the accident, I did little dating in high school and none while I was in the hospitals. That changed at M.S.O.E. It was an all-men's school, not so much by rule or tradition, but more by the total emphasis on an engineering education. There were no social fraternities, no intercollegiate sports, no dorms, and no dining hall. The student body was made up of a lot of older men on the GI Bill of Rights. Most were married. Few girls wanted to go to school for engineering, much less attend an institution that had no social activities.

The single men in the all-male school body found the all-female hospital nursing schools to be a great place to find dates. There were generally networks of men attending M.S.O.E. and dating women at the nursing schools to arrange dates from all of the hospital nursing schools in the greater Milwaukee area.

Jennifer attended the Deaconess Hospital Nursing School. We met when the nurses held a mixer and invited the students from M.S.O.E. I and several of my friends, one who had a car, went to the mixer. Although I didn't dance, I met this girl and faked it. Her name escapes me now, but halfway through the evening, she introduced me to Jennifer.

I was young and naive; I never discovered what Jennifer was. We were married two years later when she graduated from her nursing program. She worked as a nurse for one of the hospitals near Marquette University. We lived in an apartment building close to the bus lines that ran on both State and Wells Streets.

I graduated approximately six years later from my work-study program. My first work offer came from the GM plant in Doraville, Georgia. My first job description was Junior Maintenance Engineer. Our first home was an apartment complex on Buford Highway, a short way from the plant. She found work in a doctor's office some distance from where we lived. We had become a two-car family.

It would take a book to catalog all that went wrong between us. As I sat there on that small perch, I remembered the frustrations we both felt. The money wasn't good enough, the job wasn't fulfilling, she had no relatives close by and my disabilities got to her.

"How ya doin' today?" It was Riley again. He had a way about him of startling me as he came up behind me while I was deep in thought.

"Just fine," was my reply. "I didn't see you back there this morning."

"Can't get off o' work, but I'll be here Thursday and Friday."

"I saw a very large buck come across the field this morning," I said.

"He's an old one; we've been trying to get him for years. He's figured out just how far away he has to be to tease us and not get shot. He's a trophy deer; he's too tough to eat in any way but in burgers," replied Riley. "When will John be here?"

"He called early this morning. He will be in Mexico all week and won't even be here for the weekend," I replied. "He said for someone to use his stand if they wanted to."

"Someone probably will; at least Thursday and Friday, and maybe Sunday," answered Riley.

As Riley began walking away, I unloaded my gun. With these new gloves, my hands were toasty warm, and I didn't drop a single shell in the snow. I came down from the stand and walked to my car. The snow in the driveway to nowhere had warmed during the sunny part of the day and now was icy. The Sable slid around a little as I backed it out onto the road. *I will have to watch how I park tomorrow.* The weather was a little warmer, and I got heat almost immediately on my drive back to Janesville.

Back in the motel room, I checked the Weather Channel to see what to expect. The Canadian low had moved to the south, bringing some warmer weather behind it. The low for that night was only expected to reach 15 degrees. In Atlanta, the low was expected to be 35.

After cleaning up and changing into comfortable clothes, I propped up a pillow against the headboard of the bed, reclined against it, and began my quest for the day's news. I was set, with a copy of *USA Today* on my lap and the TV channel set on CNN. I must have dozed off, as the next thing I heard was the phone on the bedside stand loudly ringing. Groggily, I reached for the phone, knocking the receiver onto the floor in the process. Finally, I got my wits about me and answered the call. Linda's voice was on the other end.

She was only on the line with me long enough to tell me she was in the lobby. I remembered she said she was going to call me at 7:00, but after acting so stupidly at the library, I never expected her to follow through (third surprise of the day). I checked the clock on the bed stand. She had called on time all right.

That was quite some nap I had just taken! I had to gather my thoughts for a moment before speaking. I asked her to give me a minute and I would be right down. I was hungry. *Maybe she knew a good place to eat, and I could talk to her across a meal.* Of course, any place where she was known was probably out of the question, as she would not be with her husband. I decided to ask her what she wanted to do.

"Hi," I said to her as I rounded the corner from the elevators. She was standing by one of the chairs in the lobby. She was facing away from me, looking off toward the entrance doors to the motel. As I spoke, she turned toward me.

"Hi," she said.

"A good salesman always takes his client out to eat. That is one of the best places to do business, and the atmosphere is much more relaxed over food than just an empty table," I said.

"What does a bad salesman do?" she jokingly asked.

"About the same thing, but he is not as successful at it."

"Food sounds like a good idea," she responded.

I walked over to the chair where she was standing, and together we walked toward and then through the doors she had been so intently watching and then silently to my Hertz car. In the Sable, the conversation became more relaxed.

"Isn't this a kind of risky thing to do, to come and visit a virtual stranger while your husband is three hundred miles away trying to put food on the table?" I asked.

"I'd like to think of it more as meeting up with a long-lost friend I haven't seen in forty years."

"It sounds good to me," I replied. "Do you live in Edgerton or one of the other towns around here?"

"We bought the farmhouse and some of the buildings of an old farm on a road off Highway 106 near Bussyville. I thought country living would be great."

"You think differently now?" I asked.

"It is terribly lonely in the country. There isn't an inhabited house within a mile, and at night you can look off in all directions and not see the lights of any other farmhouse through the brush. It is so isolated," she responded.

"I have never lived in an area so desolate. I have always been in a neighborhood where you have to put up a fence to gain a little privacy. I have what was known when I bought it as a Georgia split, a tri-level house. I am on about an acre of land with more than sixty trees, and my neighbors still can wave at me as I go in and out of my front door."

We had begun to drive south on I-90 toward Beloit. There was sort of an awkward silence in the car. What does one talk about after forty years? The weather is good for a couple of sentences. We had just mentioned where each of us lived. Back to food.

"Do you have a place in Beloit where you would like to go to eat?" I asked.

"Nowhere in particular," she answered.

"Do you go ever go down to Rockford to eat?" I asked.

"No," came her reply.

"Then it is settled. We will drive to Rockford, find some restaurant that is open on a Monday night, and eat whatever their specialty happens to be." This decision made, I turned to another tack for the conversation. "What does your husband do for a living?"

"He is a printer for a printing company in Madison. He commutes in every day, which means he leaves early and comes home late," she answered.

"Has he been at that trade a long time?" I questioned. This was becoming more like twenty questions than a conversation. Somehow, I would have to do more than crack the ice, no matter how cold the water was. *Why did she come to meet me anyway?* I thought to myself. *She must have had a reason.*

After a pause, she answered. "He wasn't always a printer. He started out with high expectations and tried a number of things before printing, but that was the one he has stuck with. The pay is pretty good, but I still have to work at the library to make ends meet. Not that I don't like my job, but I had always hoped for something better. But then, what is there to do around Edgerton, Milton, Jefferson, or any of the other little towns around here? Even Madison is not a good place to work unless you work in the university system. The competition from the students for jobs tends to drive down the wages and benefits. I just don't know!" She fell silent.

How do you answer this? The frustration coming through her voice was something I had not anticipated, and here she was telling me, an almost-stranger. I thought about this for a while and came up with nothing to say, and the silence held. One Beloit exit went by, and then another, and we were on I-90 and I-39 headed for Rockford, Illinois. I decided to change the tone of this ride and try to turn it into a homecoming celebration.

"Do you remember the fun we used to have with the old gang on nights like this when we would go ice-skating at Central Park? It was so cold then, yet those are some of my warmest memories. Or the years we met at the Rialto theater and those rides in that old Hudson, taking the entire gang home after having hot chocolate and marshmallows. My mind has brought those memories to the surface at times when I have needed a lift. Those memories and the warm feelings they have generated always brought me into a better mood. Then, sometimes when I am driving along alone in a car, I think about my old friends and wonder what ever became of them. John and I moved away. What happened to the rest? Are any of the old gang still around? But John still keeps in touch with some people here, so some of our friends must be here."

We had entered Illinois and were coming up to a tollbooth, so I began scrambling around in my pockets to produce the correct change. Linda held her hand out, so I gave it to her to hold. We talked back and forth about the tolls and the condition of the roads. We exited from I-90 to I-39. We exited at one of the Rockford exits off I-39. We drove up the road a mile or two and found a pizza place open.

We entered, and the waiter showed us to a walnut-stained wooden booth. Linda sat down and slid to the center of the bench-type seat; I sat down and slid into the booth so I could sit directly across from her. This was not the kind of place I had in mind. It had a candle in the middle of the table, which was more atmosphere than I desired. A swag lamp with a fake Tiffany glass shade hung over the table. The light was so dim I almost had to ask for a flashlight to read the menu. The menu was rather complete; along with the pizza, spaghetti and meatballs, and other things, the menu also offered wine, beer, and soft drinks.

I immediately motioned to a waiter, who looked like the stereotypical pimple-faced kid. When he came to the table, I ordered a small carafe of red wine. While he was getting that, we looked the menu over and chose what we wanted to eat. The waiter came with the carafe and the two wine glasses, poured each of us a glass, and asked if we were ready to order. I gave him Linda's order. While I was giving him my order, she drank almost the whole glass of wine. The waiter refilled it, and she sipped a little more. He told us that the order would take approximately twenty minutes to prepare and we could order some appetizers to fill the gap. I looked at Linda, who shook her head no.

As soon as he left, Linda began to speak. "You and your need for speed and danger!"

I felt cutting anger in her voice.

She continued. "Do you know what you did to us? Oh! I know you suffered and were in pain and you handled that. But the rest of us... you, going over with that bike, not getting clear. Do you know how that affected me and the others? There you were on the ground, fire all around you, someone running to you with a fire extinguisher, not running fast enough!

"Do you know what you did? You were my white knight. All little girls have a white knight. I knew that the time would come when the two of us would find each other. It was my dream. It is the dream of every girl to have a friend, to be with that friend, to want to be with him more than with all other friends. That was what you were to me. Then, in April, on a street corner, in front of my eyes, you died. I saw the flames. They were all around you. Then there were people, people forming a ring around you like around a bonfire! And there was noise, the roar of the fire, and the people shouting orders to other people. You know what I did? I went home before they even put you out. To me, you had died. When I heard the reports from the hospital, I knew you were dead. You were just too stubborn to give in yet. All those months, the shock, the horror, the nightmares, the shattering of my dreams, the tears shed for those dreams and for you! To me, you were dead! How could you do that to me?"

She had tears in her eyes now. Still, she went on. "How my love turned to hate. How I hated you for what you had done to me. You changed my life when you died out there on that pavement. I even had fantasies of going to your grave and shouting obscenities over it. I saw you die and believed you dead. I couldn't go look at those charred remains. It wasn't until at the dinner table when my father brought up the accident that I knew you were still alive. He said what a shame that such a nice boy had such an accident. I supposed he thought that was what I wanted to hear. I couldn't say anything. I left the table crying and didn't join my parents 'til after school the next day when my mother and I talked a little. Then I was just waiting for you to die. I knew you would die because I saw you burn, but you didn't. And you got better. Through all of that, John kept telling me what your progress was and asking that I go with him to see you. I'm sorry. I just couldn't. Then, to see you back at school...but enough time had past, and I was not grieving for you anymore. I had grown up and become cynical. I had gone on with my life. You did that to me! You did that to me.

"But in some childish way, I hated you for what you had done to me. I still have never forgiven you for it. You got over it and have gone on to make something of yourself. I am stuck here, assistant to the librarian, dream after dream shattered!"

I sat there, stunned! I, a salesman, who lived by words his whole life, for the second time in one day was without words, having no idea what to say. Being struck dumb by the immensity of what I had just found out, I remained silent.

Fortunately, the waiter arrived with the food in the nick of time. I was still trying to think of something profound and relevant to say when I muttered, "Linda, I had no idea. I didn't know. I am so sorry."

We sat and ate in silence. I had no words to say, and she had said what she had to. I sipped my wine and offered her more from the carafe. She held out her glass and steadied it with her other hand as I poured the last wine into it. She sipped at it, and we finished eating. The place was nearly empty, although it was barely 9:00 p.m. I asked the waiter if he would mind if we sat and talked for a while. He said they closed at 10:30, but usually got the late rush at about 10:00. I thanked him for the information, and he left.

"Linda, let me tell you a story about a young boy who liked a girl very much, a boy too shy, who lacked the confidence to tell her. This boy was adventuresome, excited by danger. He stupidly tried to impress her with a feat of speed and daring. The speediest thing he saw was a motorcycle, and the most daring thing he could think of was riding very fast. One day, in an April long ago, he saw a chance to do something very daring or foolish, depending on one's perspective. No one else would take the ride. He did, and he goaded the driver to show off. It ended forever his ability to ride a motorcycle, and it drove from him the one person he tried to impress that day. He never knew why, and he never went back to find out. One day, in a hall, he heard someone give an answer he took to mean he was unreliable, unwise, and unworthy. He took it to heart and never pursued it again with her. He didn't have such lofty dreams—his were much more humble—but they too were crushed under the weight of that tipped bike. And in all the years, he had never known why."

"Why would this person you are talking about not tell that other person how he felt?" she asked.

"Because neither of those people exists anymore; each of those people is from a dream, and that dream is over forty years old," I answered. "If I were to stand at the other side of the room and look at the two of us sitting here, I would see two old people just getting acquainted for the first time. I would not see the ghosts of the past that have haunted us for these years. I wouldn't have perceived how my heart jumped when I heard your voice in the library. I would not have felt the excitement I felt when we talked. I wouldn't have felt the embarrassment I felt when I almost left the library without what I came for. I would not see the memory of the five years of my youth that warmed me."

We sat in silence for quite a while, as this was all sinking slowly in. She had opened up to me, telling me what she must do to put her ghosts to bed, and I had countered with feelings that may have opened up an area that should never have been touched.

I reached into my pocket for money to leave as a tip. "Let's pay the bill and go back," I said as I slid from the booth and stood at the end of the table.

She slid toward me, and I gave her a hand to help her from the booth. "I think going back is a good idea," she said.

I paid the bill, and we walked silently to the Hertz Sable. I unlocked the passenger's door and held it open for her. She unlocked the driver's door so I could get in easily. The night was clear, the moon was full, and the weather was warming as we headed back up the expressway to Janesville.

We talked a little about the mundane things in life—nothing of importance, just the polite little bits of conversation that grease the social order.

As we were driving into the motel parking lot, she asked, "Are you upset with me for what I said tonight? I need to know because I feel so foolish about it now."

"I have never been upset with anyone who has delivered bad news or the truth to me. I think you had to say what you said to clear up an old wound. If you can forgive me for my youth and stupidity, that is all I can ask." At that point, I concluded she had done to me what she had come to do and I would never see her again.

"Can we start this night over again tomorrow?" she asked. "Maybe at the same time and the same place?"

Now, you figure this out. I had been soundly thrashed or trashed, whichever way you wanted to look at it, and now she wanted to start this over again? What am I not getting here? "I have a better idea," I interjected. "Why don't I pick you up at your place and we eat at a very special place in Milwaukee."

"I can go for that," she replied.

She drew a map to her farmhouse on the back of the pizza place receipt. I played the part of the gentleman, opening her door for her and helping her out of the Sable. She handed me the freshly drawn map and showed me how to read it. We walked over to her car; I stood by as she unlocked the door, got in, started the engine, and drove out of the motel parking lot.

I came up to my room, and here I am at the end of a most surprising day.

Ghosts from Milwaukee Visited

It was late Tuesday night when I got back from Milwaukee. The message light on my telephone was blinking, but it was late, and I decided to answer it in the morning, but I am getting ahead of myself again.

I got up Tuesday morning at 5:30 a.m. and watched the Weather Channel to get a feel for what would happen today. Good news for the hunters, and questionable news for the deer, although the deer seem to out smart me in any weather. The high for the day would be in the low to mid thirties. The low would be in the mid-twenties with light to medium snow with accumulations from three to six inches.

I dressed for the hunt and went to the Sable to get my usual early start. I stopped at the quick stop for my morning coffee and roll and headed to the field. I checked out the ice on the driveway to nowhere and pulled in so as to avoid, if possible, getting stuck. It was warmer, and I had some hope that this would make the deer restless and get them moving. I got to my stand and decided to again stay low in the bushes. I climbed up the stand to see if the orange vests had arrived or not. I didn't expect them to have come. So far, I was right.

I had a greatly confusing night last night, and I was slightly tired when I sat down in the little nest I had made yesterday beneath my stand. As I sat there, I kept nodding off, and I just couldn't seem to keep even one eye open. I tried thinking about various things that happened so long ago when I had lived here. I thought about last night. That ghost of the past was apparently confronted and buried along with the wonder of its mystery, as it was no longer stimulating to my mind. Maybe, just maybe, this trip back was necessary to finally put things in order. I thought about the trip coming up tonight, but even the excitement of that could not keep me awake.

I sat and dozed off and on until the sun looked as though it had to be 10:00 a.m. I was about to look at my watch when I looked up, and through the weeds I saw there, in the field in front of me, a buck and a doe. Again, I saw them pawing the snow cover from the ground and nibbling on the grasses underneath. I should have been ready for them, but if I had been awake, would they have ventured this close? I thought, *Maybe if they look away for an instant, I can get to my gun. Fat chance. As soon as I move, they will be gone.* The buck turned, and he and the doe began to slowly walk toward the other corner of the field.

I grabbed my gun, but in bringing it around to my shoulder, I hit my glasses and sent them flying somewhere in the snow. I clicked off the safety, which the buck heard, and as he turned to react, I followed with a quick shot. I aimed as well as I could without my glasses and watched the buck duck and run. I missed with my second shot too. So much for my exciting morning! I was never much of a fisherman, but I thought my skills as a hunter would exceed those of the fisherman I am not. And that was an easy shot, too! It was close, and the buck was a large one.

I found my glasses, unloaded the weapon, and headed back to the Sable. I was able to back out of the driveway with no trouble. When I got to my room in the motel, I posted the Do Not Disturb sign on the door and lay down to nap. I awoke at about one-thirty and got on the phone to the John Ernst Cafe in Milwaukee, but there was no one to take the reservation. The recorded voice on the phone said they open for reservations around 4:00. At least I had gotten enough sleep that I would not fall out of the stand in the afternoon.

I left the motel and got a quick bite to eat; no more stomach trying to eat its way out. There were some clouds in the sky, but the moisture front predicted by the Weather Channel definitely had not arrived yet.

I drove to the driveway to nowhere and carefully parked the Sable. It would do no good to let it slip off the side of the driveway to end up in the ditch and spoil my dinner plans for tonight.

I made my way to the stand and climbed on top. I looked around and spotted the orange vests. By this time, I was even able to identify Riley's cap from this distance. I spent the afternoon faithfully watching for the deer. I did not sleep. I stayed alert. Everything was done perfectly right for once, and guess what? You guessed it! No deer anyplace to be seen.

Due to the lack of action, I left the stand early, making sure I had Riley's attention before I left so he would know it was me moving across the field. I got to the Sable. There had been a little more melting, but I was able to move the car onto the highway with no problems.

I called ahead to the John Ernst Cafe for a booth and got the person taking reservations. He said that tonight would be slow, but he would look for me at around 8:30 and make sure a booth was available. I thanked him and hung up.

I arrived at her house at 6:00. The house was one of the stately, old, frame houses you couldn't afford to build anymore. It appeared, in the dim light, to be sided with white-painted clapboard siding very common on old farmhouses. The main section was a square approximately forty feet at the base and two stories tall. The first floor had a picture window centered on the wall facing the road. There were two windows on the second floor above and to either side of the picture window. The roof formed a gable at this end of the house.

An added-on section attached to one of the sides was rectangular, extending approximately forty feet from where it attached. It was narrower than the other part and was indented approximately five feet to form a porch in the L shape caused by the indentation. This porch, accessible through two doors, one in the original section and one in the addition, was facing the road. A picture window was centered on the first floor looking out onto the porch. There were two windows again in the second floor. The eaves of the roof began at the tops of the second floor windows, as the roofline was now parallel to the road with the gable on the end. The lower roofline meant the rooms upstairs in this section probably had lower ceilings.

A third section was added to the back to form a modified T with the other two sections. It also was rectangular and had a full-length porch on each side. The dimensions looked to be approximately twenty-five by thirty-five feet at the base. It was two stories high, with the upper story being more of a modified loft with two windows in dormers. Facing into the porch were two windows placed under the ones in the two dormers and an entry door centered between them. The steps up to the porch were aligned with the door.

The original woodshed on the end of this had been turned into a two-car garage. From what I could see in the moonlight, the exterior of the house was kept in the style of the times during which it was built. It gave the appearance of having been well kept.

Because it was dark, I really took no notice of the detail of the other buildings that surrounded the house. I did notice that the evergreen trees bordering the lot blocked the light from any other farmhouses near or far.

I drove into the driveway and parked the car in the driveway, with the passenger door even with the shoveled walkway leading up to the side door.

I walked around the car and up the shoveled path. I climbed the steps on the side porch, walked to the side door, and knocked. Linda came to the door and opened it. She was dressed in a red sweater and a black, full skirt. Her hair was done up in the usual way she wore it, but it looked a little more blond tonight. The color of her eyes had not changed.

I entered through the door directly into the kitchen. By today's standards, this could have been called a great room, but when this house was built, it was probably where the hired help ate. It was nicely furnished, with all the modern appliances in a kind of U-shape around a work island. The cabinets and work island were finished in a dark wood stain. The countertops and backsplash areas were finished in white ceramic tiles. The U was at the woodshed end of the room and filled two-thirds of that end of it.

There was a wall that bisected the big room that formed a smaller room, taking up the other corner of the kitchen. This was a mudroom that was entered through the garage. The walls were plaster, painted with rich, yellow enamel. The ceiling was painted white. There was a large kitchen table with a yellow-patterned Formica top. The matching chairs were made of chrome-plated bent and welded metal pipe. The chair cushions and the backrest were covered in a yellow plastic material. A phone hung on the wall by the door.

"Welcome to my humble home. May I take your coat?" she asked as I entered.

She took my coat, placed it on a hanger, and hung it someplace in the mudroom.

"This is quite some house," I replied. "You certainly have made it modern and homey. How long have you lived here?"

"We bought this about seven years ago when we finally got a little ahead. We have been working at modernizing and restoring it since we moved here. There are two rooms downstairs that have not been done yet, and the upstairs will be a whole project by itself," she explained. "I'd show you around, but there is not much to see. Pull up a chair and sit down; I still have a few things I have to do before we leave."

Just then, the phone rang. It was 6:15 by my watch, and I was concerned that we would not be able to make the 8:30 dinner reservation at the restaurant. Linda didn't bother to answer the phone in the kitchen; she went into one of the other rooms to answer it. I could hear some muffled conversation coming from the direction in which she went, but I didn't try to make out any of the words. I remained seated on the kitchen chair and just looked around the room. On the wall opposite the door I came in were two large windows and a door, all protected from the weather by the porch they looked out over. The window and doorframes were rather ornate, the kind you see on houses built around the turn of the century. Someone had taken great care in restoring them to their present glory. From what I was able to see, the kitchen looked to be the activity center for the house.

"We can go now," she stated. She had her coat on and was standing framed by the doorway to the other rooms in the house.

"I'm ready," I answered.

She went to the mudroom and returned with my coat and gave it to me. I put it on, and we went out of the door of her house to the door of my Hertz Sable. With just a few steps, we had come from an age of forgotten beauty, elegance, and peace to an age of speed, efficiency, and excitement.

As we left her driveway, I noticed the moon had become hidden by clouds, and snow flurries began to fall. I followed my plan to drive on 106 to Fort Atkinson, take 26 to Johnson's Creek, and follow what used to be Highway 30, but was now I-94, to Milwaukee. The only change to this plan came as I approached Fort Atkinson. In my youth, I remembered the drive through downtown Fort Atkinson. Sometime during the past forty years, I found they had added a Highway 26 bypass around the town. Driving the bypass helped make up for some of the time lost while Linda was on the phone.

We had been in the car a while, and the heater had done the job well enough for me to open my coat and get comfortable. We had passed Fort Atkinson and were rolling through a snow shower. I broke the ice. "Tell me about yourself."

She looked over at me and said, "There really is not much to tell. I have led a simple and boring life. You could not possibly want to hear about it."

"On the contrary; I would like to know all about what you have been doing the last forty years. And besides that, I never found you boring anytime we ever talked."

She relented and began. "You left at the end of your junior high school year, and by this time, I had begun to go steady with a guy named Bill. None of the old gang was together. Whether you knew it or not, you were the one that had the energy to hold us together. Without you, John couldn't do it. I wasn't involved with any particular group; I was more in need of a strong boy than a group. My fantasies were dead, the reality was not at all kind to me, and I met and went with a number of boys. Graduation came, and I decided to go to college. I had no idea what it was I wanted to do, but my dad put up the money, and I went to the University of Wisconsin, Madison.

"I was not motivated and had no sense of purpose. I wasn't well prepared at Edgerton to pursue an academic career, and after the first semester, I dropped out. My grades were not that bad, but I saw no future in it. Mom was sympathetic. Dad was more realistic. I came home and got a job."

"What kind of choices were you looking at then?" I asked.

"The better question would be what choices were available to me then," she responded. "I'll tell you. The majors I could have chosen were limited to teaching any subject from gym to physics and nursing. My grades probably would have precluded the other professions, as only the brightest women were ever even considered."

"Times sure have changed," I answered. "So what did you do?"

"I got a job in a grocery store as a checkout girl. I spent my nights bowling and doing other things with some of the other single working girls. That is when I met Mark. He was bowling at the same bowling alley we used. We began to date. We went together for a while and then discussed getting married. It seemed the only thing to do. All of our friends were either married or planning weddings. We talked it over and decided we each could do worse and got married. It was a marriage of convenience. It has worked out reasonably well. He has his interests, I have mine, and we have the three boys."

"How long have you been married?" I asked.

"Thirty-two years," was the reply. "We discussed having a family and decided at our age we would go for it. They came about one and one-half years apart. We named them Mark Jr., Luke, and John. Mark, Jr., works at the Fisher Body plant in Janesville, Luke works at the Stoughton Trailer, and John works with his dad printing."

"Do you have any grandchildren?"

"Not that we know of," she answered. "None of the boys are married. Girls just don't want to be housewives anymore, and they haven't found the right ones yet. But then Mark Jr. is only thirty-one; he has time yet, and the rest are younger."

"I suppose that they are quite a help around the house when they get home."

"Oh, they never have lived in the farmhouse. When we moved out of the house we rented for all those years, they decided to stay and live in Edgerton. They do come out and visit us now and then, but they don't have to put up with house rules where they live.

"Did you ever marry?" she asked. "You have not mentioned a wife, and I see your finger is still bare. You were evasive at the library, and I am curious as to how a man like you could still be single."

"It is a long story and a past I would much sooner forget. It really all goes back to the accident and the years of rehabilitation I went through. You don't do much dating in rehab. The one person I wanted to keep in touch with wasn't available, and there was no way to meet any girls outside the hospital."

"That's not fair!" she complained. "I told you how I felt, and anyway, you never asked me to come."

"I had hoped you would come as a friend, and John asked you to come as a friend. I had no idea, nor any way of knowing how I had hurt you," I replied. "Anyway, I left Edgerton and said good-bye to a town that had never really welcomed me and didn't seem to miss me when I left.

"When I got to Detroit, I was still somewhat disfigured. Guess how hard it is to find a date when you don't have good looks. You may have the best personality in the world and be the center of attention, but the shallow girls I knew at the time wouldn't be caught dead on a date with me; so much for a social life. The senior year of high school was a really bad one for me, but it did do something for me I probably wouldn't have done otherwise: it focused my energy on the study of science and made it possible for me to go to engineering school.

"After high school, I took a year off for more plastic surgery to repair the burn damage that could be easily seen. It was a tough year, but by following the doctor's orders, I healed, and the world was able to see a less scary visage.

"I was accepted at M.S.O.E. on a work-study program and spent seven years working at AC Spark Plug and eight studying at M.S.O.E. It is funny when you think about it; here we were seventy miles apart, you doing one thing, and me doing another.

"It was during my first quarter at school that I met Jennifer. She was attending nursing school and had about two years to go."

I continued telling her about the marriage and all the years Jennifer and I tried to make a go of it. She was silent the whole time I described the life we had led.

We got to Johnson's Creek, and I decided it would be a good time to stop for gas. I hadn't realized I had traveled so far. I filled up and got back on the road.

Finally, she asked, "Did you love her?"

There was a long silence as I pondered that question. We were driving now on I-94, and as I tried in my own mind to answer that question, I watched the snow falling thicker and thicker on the roadway.

"I thought I loved her," I answered. "But I was never excited to return home to her. I never thought much about her when I was away. She was never my best friend. Funny thing was, I really didn't miss her when she left. I guess I loved her after a fashion, but it was never the romantic love you read about."

After that, I didn't speak for a while. Linda was sitting there silently, looking away from me out the side window. There was enough light in the car that, at times, I could see her face reflected in the window. She seemed so deep in thought.

Eventually, she looked at me and asked, "Why didn't you have children? Didn't you think that act in itself could have brought the two of you closer together, pulling together for something you both wanted?"

Now she had finally come to the crux of my problem. How could I answer that question? I sat there and thought and thought to compose an answer, to approach the subject in a delicate way.

"The answer to that question, Linda, was what finally was at the bottom of the divorce. After the fire, they rebuilt the parts necessary to live a normal productive and satisfying life. Some parts were never able to be made right. I was sterile and could never father a child. Now the doctors think with the current microsurgery the damage can be repaired, but at my age, what is the use? It's too late. In any case, Jennifer went back to Milwaukee. I heard she married again and now has several children."

The silence in the car was only broken by the sound of the larger snowflakes hitting the windshield. We had just passed Delafield and the exit to St. John's Military Academy, and soon we would be in Milwaukee.

I reached over to turn the radio on, and Linda reached out and moved my hand away from the controls. "I only wanted to tune the FM to the Delafield public radio station," I said. "I thought that on the way home we might want to listen to the program *Music in the Night*."

"How do you know about that?" she asked.

"There was a time when commuting to Milwaukee from out here was a regular thing. That radio station was on then and should still be on tonight." She let me fiddle until I found the PBS station, and then she turned the radio off.

Now, the Sable has bucket seats in the front, with armrests for each seat in the middle. These armrests can be either down on the seat cushion or up to form a part of the seat back. When I rent the Sable or the Taurus, I normally drive with the armrests in the down position so I can rest my right arm on the one for the left-hand seat while I am driving. This had been the case since I picked up the car on Friday. I was driving with my left hand, and had my right elbow on the armrest. All of a sudden, she reached across and took my arm in her hand. Now, I have to say that this definitely got my attention.

"Have you been dating since the divorce?" she asked.

I guess it is her turn to play Twenty Questions, I thought. "To what end?" I asked.

"Isn't it pretty lonely for you not to have some female companionship?" she asked.

Now she was getting into some very personal feelings that even I didn't want to explore. I am sure there are places in everyone's mind where even they don't venture. This is true at least for me. Some of those places are just too melancholy to muck about in.

"It has been around twenty years since I have had female companionship in the most intimate sense of the word. When my wife left me, I was just beginning to get into selling Capital Equipment. It is a product sold by traveling to the user's plant and working with his engineers. You don't stay home and produce enough business to live on. The travel was the last straw. She couldn't have the children she wanted, nor the close companionship she seemed to need. I left on a trip to sell a million-dollar order, and she had to go to the wedding of one of her nephews. I was to fly up to join her when I got back from my trip. We kissed and made love before I left.

"When I got back, I found the house devoid of the things she considered hers. My airline tickets were torn to shreds, with a note that she did not want to see me up in Milwaukee under any circumstances. The note also said the pets were being taken care of by a neighbor. The first of the divorce papers were delivered by registered mail. I never saw her again. I guess she got what she needed, and I continued to travel. I found a retired couple to live in and take care of the pets, the house, and the grounds. Several years ago, the man died, but the woman still takes care of the house and hires someone to do what she can't."

"Now talk to me about dating!" she stated again. "Aren't you lonely?"

"Over the years, I have learned ways to dispel the lonely feelings. I started by being very sociable in bars, but, due to my disfigurement, I never slept around. I didn't want to avail myself of the disease that is in the general population. I soon found that the new morality either caused someone to be upset with me if I didn't or upset with me if I would.

"I tried to build up long-term relationships with women and have been used and dumped. I can be a very good friend, but my heart has been scarred to the point where love can't find it anymore."

"But, last night at the pizza place, you said you felt something for me in the library when we met," she said in a quavering voice.

"I also recognized that those feelings are some I can never acknowledge or act on. I was out of place to have even spoken of them. I can't deny them, but the truth is you are not free, and I am not whole."

At this point, I turned the car off the expressway and headed over toward the M.S.O.E. campus and the John Ernst Café. It was 8:15, and the parking lot was about half full, so I guessed that everything would be going to plan. The snow was falling faster than I realized when we were driving. The snow in the lot had to be four inches deep, which made parking the car more of a challenge.

I parked, and we entered through the front door. There before us was the long bar with the animal head trophies, the hunt horns, and the beer stein trophies hanging on the wall above. The interior of the bar area was made to look like a Bavarian hunting lodge, with the bare rafters and the uniquely carved woodwork.

The maitre d' led us to the back of the lodge to one of the private booths, where he gave me the menu and seated us. The booth was constructed of oak, with windows made of glass etched with intricate hunting scenes. The door to the booth could be closed. One could eat in private here, even in the presence of a crowd.

"What do you think of this place?" I asked Linda.

"How did you ever find this?" she asked.

"Remember, I lived in Milwaukee for over eight years. Jennifer and I would come here once a year on our wedding anniversary before we moved to Atlanta. Then we would come here one night each time we were up here for our yearly visit. It is probably why she tore up my airline ticket when she left. She didn't want to get talked into coming here one last time," I said.

"If this was where you and your wife came to celebrate, why have you brought me here?" Linda sounded hurt. "I wanted you to take me to a special place for *us* tonight. I had hoped that you wanted that too."

"This is a special place for us," I replied. "It is the first time you have been here, and you have helped me bury another ghost from the past. If it will make you feel better, I promise always now to remember this as the place you and I came to eat one year during a very lonely deer hunting season."

"You keep saying—"

She was interrupted when the door opened.

The waiter came into the booth and asked about the drink order. I discussed various things on the menu and decided on a carafe of red wine. I ordered a specially prepared beef plate for two with the appropriate side dishes. The waiter left, saying the wine would be there momentarily.

Again, she started to speak. "You keep sounding as though this will be the last time we will be together."

"Enjoy the evening with me as I mean it to be enjoyed. I have come back to a place I almost was able to erase from my mind. I have come back to Edgerton for the first time in forty years and found ghosts and skeletons all over. When I came back, I was going to hunt with John Stemple. We were staying in Janesville; we were hunting for nine days and leaving, hopefully with deer. Now I have driven through the town, driven by the home of my youth, and met the lost friend of my youth at the library. I have been so happy to have been with you, but this has unleashed forces that would have better been left alone—"

The waiter opened the door again and poured the wine. It is interesting that when the door remained closed, we talked freely, but when the door was opened, we both stopped. The waiter left, and the door closed again.

"It has been hard for me, too," she answered.

"I have a question for you. You must answer this truthfully—not that you would lie to me, but you might want to avoid the question...No, I don't want to know—at least not now. Forget I asked."

The question I wanted to ask revolved around how well she knew Mrs. John Stemple and if John or Mrs. Stemple knew that Linda worked at the library. There were many other ramifications of those questions, but for the time being, they would remain mute.

"You have really made me curious about this question," she said pensively. "Please ask."

"I want this to be a special night for both of us to remember; you out in the lonely countryside waiting for your family, and me with my lonely existence robbed of a family by my own foolishness."

The food came, and we ate. We talked about the food and the weather. The waiter looked out a window and said that it was still snowing hard. I began to think, *This will really make the local gossip if I was to have a problem getting Linda to her house.*

When we were finished eating, it was 9:10, and the snow in the lot was six inches deep. One of the waiters volunteered to get the car out of the lot for us. I tipped him, and we got in the car at the entrance door. I began driving through the new snow back toward the expressway. The snow had been plowed here, but what would it be like on 106 or the back road to where she lived? The trip back was going to take a long time, as I couldn't imagine driving fast in this snow.

As I got up on the expressway and began heading west, the white, falling snow reflecting the light from the headlights made it look as though we were traveling through a lighted tunnel. The heat from the car heater warmed us against the cold radiating through the windshield and side windows. All of a sudden, I noticed Linda had pushed the armrests between us up, making them a backrest. She moved as far over as her seatbelt would allow. Placing both arms tightly around the upper part of my right arm, she cuddled up to me and, laying her head on my shoulder, went to sleep. I leaned over and was able to use the dash controls to turn the radio on. We could hear the soft classical music coming from the NPR station.

I should have told her that she was unsafe in the seatbelt leaning like this. I should have told her it was dangerous to do this because of the airbag. I should have told her she shouldn't do this because her back would be stiff in the morning. But I didn't use any of those excuses. I should have told her to stop because it was wrong, but I liked what she was doing, and I liked the smell of her perfume. At this point, I was a weak man fishing in another man's pond and enjoying it too much to stop.

By the time we got to Johnson's Creek, the snow had subsided to just flurries and the ground cover wasn't more than three inches deep. The FM station was long gone, and I didn't try to find another. Her perfume had worked its magic on me, and I was feeling more and more amorous. By the time I got to her place, the snow was deeper and there was a wind blowing it into small drifts. I took that as being fortuitous, as it would hide the car tracks of the Sable. She had been asleep, and I had done nothing to wake her before we got to her house. When I got there, I awakened her as gently as possible. She hugged me tightly and asked if I shouldn't come in and spend the night or at the very least have a cup of coffee. I could have rationalized doing anything, but I knew the limitations of my willpower, and going anywhere near the inside of that house would have been disastrous. I said good night and good-bye, in case I didn't see her again before I left for Atlanta. I drove from her driveway using more willpower than I ever thought I had.

I made it back to the motel parking lot and went inside.

I am lying here being kept awake by the message light. I say to myself, *I guess I will have to pick up the message or I will get no sleep.* I pick up the phone and dialed zero for the operator. "Hello. What is my message?"

"Call eight-eight-four-six-five when you get in," the operator says.

I dial, and, immediately, the phone rings and is answered. "Hello." It is Linda's voice.

"Hello. It's Peter. Is anything wrong?" I ask.

"I just wanted to know you were back safely," she responds. "What took you so long? I have been sitting here by the phone since you left, and I was concerned you were in the ditch somewhere."

"No. I just took my time getting here," I answer.

"I guess I knew you would be okay, but I wanted to hear your voice. Tonight was a wonderful night, and I wanted to tell you how much I enjoyed it."

"I had a wonderful time too." I don't know what to say. I feel like a schoolboy again, and, worst of all, I like the sound of her voice on the line too. Somehow, I can still smell her perfume.

"I'll be alone for Thanksgiving dinner," she says. "I'm sure there will be few places for you to eat, as most places close. I want you to come over, and I'll fix something."

"Don't you have someplace to go? I am sure you couldn't have planned to eat alone on Thanksgiving. Someone must have invited you," I reply.

"Generally, I am alone, as the boys are usually away hunting, and this has been going along this way for years," she answers. "Anyway, I want your company on that lonely day."

"Is this dinner as in lunch, or as in supper?"

"As in supper," she replies. "Come as you are right out of the field. You can wash up in the mudroom."

"Okay," I say. "What do you hear from the boys in the woods?"

"He called just before we left for Milwaukee. They haven't seen anything yet. He calls every night at about 6:00 before they all go out drinking. I get my update then," she answers.

"I will be at your house right after the hunt on Thanksgiving Day then," I say.

"Can I call you tomorrow night, after say 7:30?" she asks.

"Okay. I'll be here," I reply.

"Bye."

"Bye." I hang up the phone.

Edgerton at Night

It is Wednesday night, and I am headed to bed. It is not early, but I still hope to be in the field at dawn, snow permitting.

My day began as usual here in Janesville, with a 5:30 wake-up call from the front desk. I opened my eyes, got out of bed, and peeked out the window at the snow on the ground. I turned on the cable TV Weather Channel. The weather person said the temperature was about twenty-three degrees Fahrenheit, the wind was calm, and snow was predicted—about three to six inches. It should begin about midmorning and last until about 10:00 p.m. This could keep the deer from moving. Good news deer, bad news hunters.

I headed for the bathroom and began the morning clean-up and shaving ritual prior to the dressing for the hunt.

I went over to the window again and looked around at all of the snow. I decided that Riley and the orange vests wouldn't be out there. I was a bit—no, a lot—tired from last night, and sitting out there dozing in the snow and cold really didn't appeal to me.

I lay back down on the bed, pulled the covers up around my neck, and within moments, I was back asleep. I had wimped out! But when I awakened at noon, I felt a lot better. I expected Linda was at the library on time and would nap after work. I looked out the window at the falling snow and checked the Weather Channel for an update. They had it right;

it was still snowing. The forecast depth had changed though; it now was to be six to nine inches of snowfall for the day. The front had somehow slowed and was picking up more moisture from somewhere—Atlanta, probably. I dressed for the hunt, spoke to the desk clerk on the way out, cranked up the Sable, picked up an Arby's to-go, and headed for the stand.

I pulled into the driveway to nowhere and parked. The snow was falling at a pretty fast rate and had deposited at least five inches of snow over the snow already on the ground. I hoped I had parked the car wheels to miss the ice now buried under all that snow.

When I got to the stand, I checked for the orange vests. None were to be seen. I decided to make the best of it and went back to the car, where I got the tarp I bought to protect the paint on the car when and if I got lucky and had to take the deer I killed to be registered. Back at the stand, I opened the tarp and draped it over the top of the stand. With the small rope and knife I now carried in my hunting clothes, I fashioned a tent-like structure to keep the falling snow off. I guessed it was time to give Riley and the orange vests something more to talk about and laugh at. After all, I had been behaving myself since Saturday morning, and that was a long time to have deprived them of humor.

By the time I got everything arranged, it was already 3:00. I cleaned the fallen snow out of the nest I had made earlier in the week and I sat down behind the ladder, being shielded from the falling snow by the makeshift tent overhead, and awaited the coming of the deer. I waited and waited and waited. Now that I had a watch I could easily read, I checked it often.

A note to the wise sitting at a stand: a watched clock never boils. Now, that statement may be dumb, but no one can doubt the truth of it. But seriously, time seemed to stand still as I sat there watching the clock.

To kill time, I began to think of the summer after fourth grade. Sometime between the end of school and July 4, a carnival would pull into town and set up in Central Park. A house on the edge of the park, if my memory is still working right, was the headquarters for the Edgerton VFW post. It was built so the basement opened onto a portion of the park. Some doors opened to form a counter from which they could sell beer.

John had worked hard and had talked his mom—she was easier to convince than his dad—into letting him stay in town at my house for that celebration. He and I were going to hang around the park on Friday night and Saturday. We didn't have much money to spend, but we were going to watch the way things worked. Well, on Friday night, as we were walking around looking at things, one of the men at the post asked if we would like to earn some money. We said we would. The man said he would give us $2 each if we would come back at 8:00 in the morning and pick up trash. We said we would be there.

Sometime later, Linda and her friends arrived, and we, as a kind of loose group, moved around the midway. I had a lot of fun that evening just being with all my friends. It was that informal gang that just got along together. Nothing was planned; it just happened.

We were there at 8:00 the next morning, and, sure enough, there was the man ready to put us to work. We worked 'til noon, just picking up paper and trash from the midway and the grounds around the park.

By opening time, 1:00 in the afternoon, the park looked good. We walked to my place, and Mom fixed us lunch. After lunch, we went back to the park, but the mystery and excitement had been lost during the clean-up. We decided we were bored with the carnival and went over to Saunders Creek, which runs through the center of the park. We always thought it fun to lift and move the stones in the water to catch the crayfish that lived under them. Later in the afternoon, Linda and her friends ended up cheering us on in our quest for the little creatures. Who knows how much damage to the balance of nature and the food chain we did that afternoon, but we played there regularly.

In front of us boys, the girls would never do such a unladylike thing as hunt crayfish, but one Saturday later in the summer, Linda and several of her friends were in jeans rolled up to the knees, barefoot in the water, just pestering the heck out of the crayfish. I watched from a distance. If they saw me, they didn't let on, and I decided it would tarnish the image they tried to project if I were to go and join them. Or maybe, just maybe,

I was afraid they would outdo me and I would lose my pseudo-macho image. You can play it either way, and it works.

In some respects, I think when John suggested this deer hunt that from deep in my subconscious came the desire that he and I were going crayfish hunting. Or maybe the memory of all the fun things he and I did when we were growing up together came through my subconscious. I will never know why I said yes to coming deer hunting, but never in my wildest dreams, did I ever think Linda would become a part of this, as she had so many times so many years in the past.

The time was 4:30, and as I looked over my shoulder through the falling snow, I saw Riley walking across the field at his usual gait. Well, I deserved whatever he had to say. After all, it was kind of wimpy to have put up a tent to keep the snow off. I don't think it was illegal, but it could have been. Riley was halfway across the field when a shot rang out in the woods past the fenced tree line to my right.

No shots followed, and no bullets zinged by me, to my great relief. Riley changed his course and headed to the little woods. I finished folding my tent, tucked it under a rung of the ladder, unloaded my gun, and headed toward the corner of the fence. Halfway there, I reached the break through the fence and went across it to Riley's side. We walked together past the corner, alongside the woods, and up a little hill. There, we found one of Riley's orange-vested friends with a medium-sized buck on the ground.

Once we got to where the buck lay, Riley said, "Good thing you avoided that corner there," as he pointed to the corner we had just passed. "Full of poison ivy. Probably wouldn't hurt you now, as it's frozen, but good idea to avoid it."

"Thanks," I said.

"Quite the construction ya had for the snow this afternoon."

"Thought I'd be creative. I kinda liked it."

"Leave it to ya city guys to improve on Mother Nature and do the strange thing," he countered.

"Just trying to make your job more interesting," I said jokingly.

"Well, ya sure are doing that!"

I stood around the deer with the other orange vests while the one who shot the buck field dressed him. Now I had seen it done, and with the Xeroxed instructions I had, I should have no problem doing my own buck when I get him. When he had the deer field dressed, he took a small, plastic bag from one of his pockets and laid it on the snow. Then he reached inside the carcass and cut out what I was to learn were the tenderloins. These he placed in the plastic bag, which he placed in his pocket. This done, he pulled a rope from another pocket, looped it around the rack, and began to tow the carcass over the little hill in the woods to the field overlooking buildings along the highway. He said Marty wouldn't mind them picking up the deer there, and they wouldn't have to lift it over the fence. I was told another orange vest had already made the walk to bring a truck to Marty's to pick up the deer to take it to be registered and properly tagged.

I walked to the Sable a different way, following the fencerow on Marty's side to the road and then walking up the road to the driveway to nowhere.

By now it was pretty well dark, and with the snow falling the way it was, I decided I would have to hurry to get to the motel in time to receive my phone call.

The snow began to fall faster as I drove through Indian Ford. *They will have to do something about that politically incorrect name!* It seemed as if the sky was falling by the time I got to Janesville and into my motel room. Actually, the state of Wisconsin seemed to handle the snow on the roads rather well. Rock County seemed to be doing a good job also, as all the roads I took had been plowed and were in great shape for the amount of snow that had fallen. As a practical matter, if that amount of snow had fallen in Atlanta, it would have tied the city up in knots for three days minimum.

The time was 7:00; she was going to call at 7:30. No time to go and get something to eat until after she called. I did my best to get out of my clothes and into the shower and was just drying off when the call came.

"Hello?" I said. I was standing beside the bed still dripping water when I picked up the receiver.

"Hi," was the response from the other end.

"I just got out of the shower," I said. "I have no clothes on. Can I call you back in five minutes?"

"It isn't proper to talk on the phone unless you are dressed," she said with a chuckle in her voice.

"I'm not worried about it being proper, but the room isn't that warm. I am still dripping water, and I actually have goose bumps. I'll call right back," I said as I hung up the phone.

This is something, I thought as I was dressing. *Telling someone on the phone that you are naked. Where is your sense of decorum anyway? What will she think of you?* I guess being single all these years has affected me, as I don't know how to talk to a lady. I could have said something like, "Give me time to dress," or "Just let me call you back in five," but no, I got truthful and explicit. Now that I was dressed, I sat down on the edge of the bed, picked up the phone, and dialed her number. I still had it from early this morning. The phone rang several times before she answered.

"Hello," she said.

"Hi," I said this time.

"How was your hunt today?" she asked.

"One of the orange vests shot an eight-point buck," I answered. "How was your day?"

"The snow kept most people away, so I came home at noon. That took care of the slippery road problem," she answered.

"How are the roads out by you?"

"Highway106 was plowed and in good shape, but my road is a little iffy right now," she answered.

"Will you get out of your driveway?" I asked.

"Should be no problem," she answered. "One of the neighbors comes by to plow it if the snow is over four inches deep. He should have it plowed buy 10:00 tonight. I'm okay if I keep my car in the garage. That is why I came home early. I usually do when it snows a lot during the day."

"Have you heard from your hunters up north?" I asked.

"They called at 6:00. They are snowed in and had to spend the day in town. Couldn't even get to the woods."

"That's too bad," I said.

"What are you going to do tonight?" she asked.

"I still have to go out and eat," I responded. "After dinner, I guess I will just sit around the room and kill time. What are you doing tonight?"

"I'll be fixing the turkey for the dinner tomorrow. I have a small one and will cook it along with a ham and other fixings," she answered.

"How come so much meat for just two people?" I asked.

"Tradition. I always do this and then pack sandwiches from it until Christmas. Then I do it again at Christmas and eat from it until Easter."

"All this talk of food is makin' me hungry, and you have to get on with making the food, so I guess I had better say good-bye."

"It was so good to hear your voice again," she said, and she hung up the phone.

I placed the receiver in the phone cradle and sat on the edge of the bed looking at the phone for a little while. Was I feeling pangs of loneliness? After all these years of working so hard, was the great stone heart showing signs of softening?

I remember when Jennifer left there were a few times when I would come home to the empty house and feel alone and dejected. When I got the live-in caretakers for the house, those feelings slowly went away. For a while on the road, I would get very lonely and go out to drink and find companionship in bars, but that was short-lived. I found that by working long hours I became too tired to be lonely.

I had dated women, but nothing ever worked out. They were either using me for some purposes or they were put off by my disfigurement. Some had wanted children and, naturally, that problem also precluded a relationship. I had accepted the reality of my situation and had learned how to live without being lonely. The secret was work, work, work, and more work. I became too busy to be lonely and too tired to care.

Now here I was settled in a motel room in Janesville, Wisconsin, a snowstorm happening outside, and no work to do. I have never found TV to be a salve for loneliness. By and large, it just points out what I have missed in life. There was a time when fast cars gave me joy, but no longer. When I go to a restaurant to eat, I must find one where families don't go. Sitting alone at a table and waiting to be served with a family at the next table is too much for me to take. Having been in that type of situation has depressed me for days, and I now know how to avoid it.

I was in good shape until Monday, when I ran across Linda in the library. Now, tonight, I have an emptiness eating at me that I haven't had for twenty years, and I can't think of a way to combat it. This heart of stone wants to get in the car and drive to her house just to be near her. What a silly thought! She is married and has a family. She is an old friend. Don't damage the relationship by acting foolish. And yet, last night, she slept with her head on my shoulder for the better part of two hours. The night before, when it would have made the greatest sense to have said good-bye, she asked to see me again and start over.

It was then, if I had been wise, that I should have said let us bury the old ghosts and part friends, yet, deep in my heart, I guess I wanted to see her again. I wanted somehow to let her fill a little corner of this heart of stone. Now she has put a crack in it that will take a long time to repair.

Maybe if I go out to find a bar I can sit and have something to eat and enjoy my surroundings. In that vein, I got up from the bed, put on the only warm coat I brought from Atlanta, and went to the Sable. I drove around Janesville for a while without ever finding what I would have called a neighborhood bar. Then my memory came through like a flash. Hadn't I seen a sign on West Fulton Street in Edgerton that read Oats Bin and advertised live entertainment? *I think I will drive there and check it out*. I did do one wise thing, though, before I left Janesville: I stopped at an Arby's and got a roast beef sandwich.

The roads were still pretty good when I got to Edgerton. I parked the Sable across the street in the empty lot that looked like it could be a parking lot hiding under snow. It had other cars and trucks parked on it in a fairly haphazard way, and there were no price tags on them, so I knew it was not your average used car lot. I walked across the street and entered the Oats Bin.

By Atlanta standards, and even by Detroit standards, I would have called this place a dive. But once my eyes got accustomed to the lack of light and the fog cleared from my glasses, I concluded it had a definite charm all of its own. Apparently, there was no show going on during this week night, as the stage area was empty. I just ambled in, trying to blend in with the crowd. I thought this should be enough diversion to get her off my mind. Then I realized that if I thought of her first and this place second, already I had failed.

I looked down toward the end of the bar, and in his deer-hunting clothes with his special hat on his head sat Riley with his back to me. I moved down the bar, taking pains to keep my head turned away from the table where Riley and the orange vests were seated. In the background, I could hear comments from some others in the bar.

"How'd that guy sound again?" someone asked.

"Thought I'd be creative. I kinda liked it," was Riley's reply as he was trying to mimic how I sounded.

Everyone at that end of the room laughed at his interpretation of my Southern drawl. I couldn't help but laugh myself.

"Tell us again about the t—t—tent he put up today to keep the snow off," someone stuttered.

Riley went into a long dissertation, explaining the way in which I had constructed the thing using my stand as the tent pole.

About this time, the bartender came over to me and asked what I wanted to drink.

"I'll have what they are drinking," I said. "They sure are having a good time with it, and maybe it will help me."

"One Miller coming up," he said as he filled the glass from the tap. "But the beer ain't what is causing all the fun though. John Stemple invited this friend of his up to deer hunt and we ain't seen such goins-on since I don't know when."

"I'm new around here; I see this stage over there. Do you book shows here?" I asked.

"On occasions we have some local talent that comes in and does a routine, but generally there is only music, and that is on the weekends," he replied.

Just then, a rather thin, old-looking man entered the bar. Some of the patrons sitting near the door began to whoop and cheer calling out

"The Prez is here." Then, from another area came a request "Sing *I wanna spear fish too!*"

At that, I turned to the bartender and asked, "Is he part of the entertainment?"

"I guess you could say that," he answered, "in more ways than one."

"The Prez," as he was called, took off his coat and hung it on a peg and began to walk over toward the stage. With his coat off, he looked even thinner than before, bordering on gaunt. His posture was that of a perpetual slouch. Just as he was about to get up on the stage, someone called him over to a table to talk.

I turned to the bartender and asked, "John isn't up yet?"

"Naw. Someone said he couldn't make it because of some business deal," was his reply.

"The Prez" was still talking to the person at the table, and the cries from the floor for his performance had quieted down.

"Aw shucks," I said, trying to sound like the folks I remembered did when I was growing up here. "I really had hoped to see John this year. I came in to see if he was here tonight." I paid for my beer, picked it up from the bar, and walked over to behind the chair where Riley was sitting.

"And he is so clumsy!" Riley was saying. "He—"

Just then, he was interrupted by someone saying, "Riley, how clumsy was he?" and as he said it, the orange vest who had shot the deer this afternoon winked at me and made a motion with his hand like I should pour my beer over Riley. I looked at him and, smiling, shook my head no.

"He...He...He..." Riley continued laughing hard but trying to stop, "was sooo clumsy he almost fell out of his stand the first day."

My friend across the table had poked another orange vest, and he too was now looking at Riley but somewhat over his head at me. Just as he was about to say something and point, I placed my finger to my mouth as to shush him and shook my head no. I hadn't had my turn yet to ask a dumb question.

"I even heard that he thought that all does had white under their tails," I said, trying to disguise my voice.

"Well he might be dumb about the woods, but I don't think he is that dumb," Riley said, not looking back at me.

"The clerk at the motel where he is staying told me that," I replied.

Riley just laughed and changed the subject. He might have thought he recognized my voice.

I wasn't into embarrassing somebody from the woods who could take a shot at me so easily. I shook my head no and made the shush sign again to the orange vests across the table and headed back to the bar. I placed my glass on the bar, said so long to the bartender, and walked back out in the snow. *Quite a place, that Oats Bin*, I thought.

I looked at the big, open place between the two buildings right there beside me. It seemed that Fritzke's Cigar Store should have been there. Ah, yet another ghost from the past. I walked up the street and turned the corner, expecting to find the old Carlton Hotel and the Rialto Theater. In my mind's eye, I saw them standing there in all of their remembered majesty. No luck; the places where they should have been were just empty lots with a nice, clean covering of snow.

As I walked back up to West Fulton Street, I looked across the street to my right and to my left. Through the falling snow, I saw the lineup of tobacco warehouses fifty feet wide, two-hundred feet long, and three stories high, with steeply peaked roofs and walls made of cream-colored brick—standing sentinels to the glory of the tobacco age, when this town was lovingly called the Tobacco City.

But, alas, I was only looking at the ghosts of a busier time, images in my mind reposing in the snow, waiting to join the other buildings of the past that are no more. In reality, I could see what remained of that lofty row of buildings: two buildings far apart, appearing deserted and as lonely as I felt. And, farther across, I could see the railroad station and the tracks all blanketed in the same snow, all with ghosts of that busier time milling about waiting for the sound of the passenger train that will never come again and the REA express truck that has so long been silent.

I walked across the street and looked back at the row of storefronts. The picture in my mind showed Wileman's Variety Store; Wikum's Bakery; Frizke's Cigar Store; the Western Auto Store; the Edgerton Store, the clothing store owned by the Springer family; the Tobacco Exchange Bank; the five and dime; the jeweler; Hain Livek and Arthur Hardware; Gambles Store; and, at the intersection of Fulton and Main, the bus terminal. I focused my eyes again and all that was gone. The storefronts were there, but all else was gone, the ghosts only staying around to be driven away by the passage of time.

The total loneliness of this town and the complete loneliness of my heart was so overwhelming that I began to walk faster to get to the Sable. I had to drive out of this void into reality on a cold snowy night when even the animals knew better than to venture out.

When I got back to reality, Janesville, I parked the Sable, got to my room, and turned on the Weather Channel. The front should be past by midnight, and the snow for the day should not exceed nine inches. The temperature tomorrow should be in the low thirties with a moderate breeze. Good news for the hunters, bad news for the deer.

A Thanksgiving Evening to Remember

Thanksgiving Day has passed, and I am back where I belong in my room here at the motel. I guess the best thing is to hit the bed and try to get some sleep. No guarantee, though, with all that has happened. I have left a wake-up call for 5:30, but there is no guarantee I'll get up.

Thanksgiving Day began as any other day this week. As I was dressing, my mind began to become active. The loneliness from last night was still fresh in my memory. I began to consider just what a special opportunity this has been to hunt deer.

Then my thoughts returned to the field, and reality set in. Hunt deer! It's like the deer are teasing us hunters; or is it us the hunters that are teasing them? Just think. Sunrise should be seen to be appreciated. This should be one of the advantages of deer hunting: the chance to sit in the deer stand to watch the sunrise. What a wonder. Sitting in the deer stand watching the sunrise and being teased by the deer all at the same time!

But aren't we smarter than the deer? If we are smarter, then we must be teasing the deer, I think. *This makes sense to think of this as teasing as opposed to hunting. Consider this: hunting implies an overt activity or action on the part of the hunter, as in to look for or find as opposed to sitting in one spot with the hope that in the course of nine days some suicidal deer will wander by, expecting to be shot.*

My mind snapped back to the real world, and I proceeded with the ritual dressing of the hunter. As I left the elevator, I gave my regards to the desk clerk and proceeded out the door to the Sable.

I changed my quick stop routine and got a coke and a small, wrapped, baked pie for breakfast. The snow had stopped, the roads had been cleared, and the trip to the driveway to nowhere was uneventful. I noticed a slight breeze blowing the snow around a little, so I anticipated it being colder than usual on the stand.

I got to the stand in plenty of time to get well situated before sunrise. The morning was going to be overcast—*so much for my brilliant sunrise*—which would help, as looking at snow on a bright day tended to tire my eyes anyway. As I looked around in the predawn light and checked out the woods behind me, I counted at least a dozen orange vests planted around my northern perimeter. If any deer were stupid enough to venture into that meadow, he would have to be very nimble to escape getting hit. I looked toward John's stand and saw an orange vest on it also. We certainly were well deployed for the maximum result.

As I sat there waiting for the deer, I thought about what had happened since I got there. Nothing was as I expected. I know that one can never go home, as the saying goes. I considered myself immune from that, as I never considered this home anyhow.

As I walked last night through the streets of Edgerton in the snow and saw in my mind the ghosts of what had been, the desolation of what is now forced me to think of what this would become. Where will this town go? What will be left in another thirty years? Will the area grow, or will it become even smaller? The touchstones of my memories were either metamorphosed into something new or gone so completely that they only existed as ghosts in the memory of a few.

Take the Carlton Hotel. Here was a building that I remembered to be bigger than life. It was a brick building with a stone front, probably one hundred feet on the front by two hundred feet on a side. It had to be at least three stories high. It had a gabled roof. The whole edifice was set back from the street far enough that there was room for a massive porch in front. The porch had to be fifty feet on the front and at least ten feet front to back. It had a flat roof with a massive stone railing around it like the crown on the head of a magnificent regent. There was a pair of large doors that opened onto the roof as though it was a porch itself. It was all supported by four stone pillars. The concrete floor of the porch was at least five feet from the ground and had massive steps that led up to it. The steps were at least ten feet wide. I remember looking up the massive stone stairs and seeing two large doors with full glass panes that, when both opened at the same time, gave me the impression of two arms opening to welcome the lucky guest inside. I imagined that the inside was as glorious as the outside appeared, but I never ever entered that hotel. I believed it was for adults and was just off limits. Now you might wonder why that building so impressed me. I guess the idea of salesmen being able to travel was mysterious and alluring to me. But there was something else that brought back the Carlton Hotel.

This was Thanksgiving Day. In my youth, this day was followed by the Saturday after Thanksgiving Day! This was one of the most sacred days in the life of the secular child awaiting Christmas. This was the day that Santa arrived in town. In New York, there was the big Macy's Christmas parade on Thanksgiving Day, and this began the Christmas buying season for the city. Other cities also must have had the same kind of celebration. Edgerton was too small for a parade. We were too small for much of anything! But the merchants could not be denied. At 2:00 p.m. on the Saturday after Thanksgiving Day, Santa would miraculously appear at the Carlton through the double doors onto the roof of the porch, having entered the motel from his sleigh parked on the backside of the roof. He would then proceed to utter, with great volume, a long string of "ho ho ho's." Then he would come to the railing with a large bag and begin to throw candy bars from the roof to the crowd of kids milling about below.

I missed this event the first year I lived in Edgerton. I heard about it and never made the same mistake again. The next years, I was part of that excitement over Santa. I was there in that crowd milling about, waiting for the rain of candy. During those years at this public event, my warmest memories were of Linda having also been attracted to the event and my being there with her.

There was a knack to getting candy. It became obvious that Santa was not very good at throwing the candy. Most of it landed very close to the Carlton Hotel porch. If you were to be successful and get any of that candy at all, you had to get there early to be in the front of the milling crowd. Of course, you had to be strong, with a good sense of balance, or the milling throng would push you down and trample you when the candy throwing began. But there were ways of handling this and we, Linda and I and the friends we had, found ways to compensate. Among other things, elbows worked well.

I looked at my watch. Time had passed quickly. I heard no gunshots. My time as watchman on the stand was complete, and I could yell with confidence, "10:05, all the deer are safe!" Now that was not exactly what I wanted to say, but that was the truth. I unloaded my weapon, taking care not to drop any more shells in the snow. I waved at the orange vests that were still in the woods around me and the one in John's stand and headed for the Sable. I figured they would have a very peaceful hunt until I returned this afternoon, as the deer seemed to be taking Thanksgiving Day as a holiday too.

As I left the driveway to nowhere, I decided to follow Highway 59 east to Edgerton. As I came around a curve in the road, I saw a business kind of hidden behind a hill. It seemed to have a sizable junkyard connected with it. There was the name Morrison connected with it. As I continued driving, I saw the sheepskin marsh was full of water. Coming into Edgerton from the west was so different than I remembered that I wouldn't have recognized it except for the sign. Last night, as I walked around the streets in town, I thought the place was dying. Now, as I drove into town from the west, I found an area of new subdivisions and houses. People born here were actually building here, and it appeared others were also moving here. What a surprise. As I drove into the center of the town, I looked with a critical eye at the business section. There was not much left of it. But what was there seemed to look healthy. I drove across 51, wondering what I would find east of town. I drove down the small hill and across Saunders Creek. The old Highway Trailer building was still there. The old hill going out of town, called New York Hill, was still there. Someone was selling antiques from the grand house that was for so many years the home of Dr. Sumner.

I decided I would drive out 59 toward Milton. I didn't think much about it, but, all of a sudden, at the edge of town, there was I-90. I turned onto it and headed back to Janesville.

Back in Janesville, I got another Arby's roast beef sandwich and went to my room to rest. *I might be a little late in getting home tonight,* I thought, *and I still have to hunt tomorrow. I must show up for the hunt tomorrow so the orange vests don't think me too much of a wimp.*

I woke up from my nap at about 2:45. I got dressed and put a change of clothes in a dry-cleaning bag I found in the motel room. I left the motel at approximately 3:00. That was a pretty good time, as it usually takes that long just to wake up from a normal nap. I waved at the desk clerk and headed for the Sable. I rushed a little, but was out and in my stand by 3:30. I decided this was going to be very serious deer teasing this afternoon. I looked over to John's stand and found the orange vest over there tied to the tree with a small rope around his chest. From where I sat, he appeared to be sleeping. I thought, *I will have to consider that for tomorrow morning if I am that tired.*

I sat and watched the area before me. I could see over the little rise in ground ahead of me to the road and the driveway to nowhere where the Sable was parked. As I sat there, I thought I saw some movement near the large, red tobacco shed across the road. As that was open farmland with no trees, there were no orange vests to be seen on that side of the road.

I watched the area intently, but was somewhat hampered by the knoll I was looking over. I was able to watch the cars as various vehicles drove both east and west. All of a sudden, there was a squealing of the brakes, and a minivan skidded sideways into the ditch. Then, from in front of where the van had skidded, came three deer headed between John's stand and mine. They had been startled by the car and were now on the run. I looked down the barrel of my gun and waited for them to continue to run my way. Then they began to veer toward John's stand. They would be out of range for me, but the orange vest in John's stand would have a good shot.

"You in John's stand!" I yelled at the top of my voice. "Coming at you at two o'clock! Take the shot!"

His head snapped up, and up came his gun. The deer kept coming his way. My yelling must have helped drive them into his sights. He fired, and the largest deer fell in its tracks. He fired again, but the next deer in line took an evasive move, and he missed. He took several more shots, but hit nothing. The old saying looks to be true. It states, shooting slugs at moving deer is as good as pitching rocks at them. I looked across the field at the van in the ditch. I looked over at the dead deer in the field. I unloaded the gun, came down from the stand, and walked to the deer. The orange vest was there, already beginning to field dress the deer when I got there.

"Thanks for waking me," he said.

"You are welcome," I replied. "I am going to see if I can lend some help to the people in the van in the ditch." I pointed that direction.

"How did that happen anyway?" he asked.

"The driver had to swerve to miss the three deer you took shots at," I answered.

"I've tagged it and am almost through gutting it. I'll join you in trying to help the people in the van," he answered.

We walked together across the field to where the van was and spoke to the driver. No one was hurt, and the van had missed hitting the deer, but the van would have to be pulled from the ditch.

"Have you a chain," I asked, "or even a strong rope?"

"No," answered the driver.

"I'll give someone a ride to the next house. Maybe someone can help," I said.

"Let me come, too," said the orange vest. "We'll go to Marty's and have him start a tractor to pull you out."

The three of us went to my car, and I dropped them off at Marty's. I then decided that it was too late to go back to the stand, said good-bye, and left.

I arrived at Linda's close to on time. When I got there, her driveway was already plowed, and the tracks showed that she had already had her car out and back in the garage. I parked kind of in the middle of the driveway, where my tracks would not easily show. I got out of the car and went up the stairs of the porch to the side kitchen door and knocked. I could hear the rustling in the kitchen as I stood waiting at the door.

When the door opened, there was Linda in a dark, blue dress with puffy sleeves, with almost bare shoulders forming an open V front, the V coming to a point in the front of the dress high enough to be modest but low enough to be interesting. The waist was tight, accenting both her upper body and her hips. The skirt was full and would probably rise quite high if she was to twirl. This was a dress that she could have fashionably worn to any New Year's Eve ball anywhere in the world. I have never heard of anyone having a Thanksgiving ball, so that would not have been a fair assessment. Her shoes were blue to match the dress, and with the dark silk stockings she wore, she reminded me of a fashion model I had a date with once. Around her neck, accented by the blue dress, was a string of matched white pearls. She was wearing soft makeup, giving the impression of no makeup at all. Her hair was the same as I had always remembered it.

In a word, she looked stunning. The soft, yellow light in the kitchen probably had something to do with the overall impression I had, but she didn't need to use tricks to look beautiful to me.

I stepped through the door still dressed in my hunting clothes. Once inside, I stepped back to take in all the beauty. I couldn't help looking at her. "You look absolutely stunning," was all I could say.

"Tonight, flattery will get you nowhere," she said jokingly. "Would you like to use the mudroom to change? I left some towels there if you wish to shower."

"Thank you," I said as I headed through the door to shower and change. "I'm warning you, the clothes I brought will pale before you, as I didn't bring a tux."

"That is all right," she said. "I don't expect we will go anywhere tonight anyway. I just wanted to dress up once for a special occasion."

I finished showering and dressing and came out of the mudroom wearing loafers with white socks, gray flannel slacks, and a white turtleneck shirt. What a contrast to the beauty standing in front of me.

"If I would have had an idea of how you would look, I would have rented a tux!" I exclaimed.

She took my hand and led me toward the formal dining room. As I got close to her, the perfume she was wearing—I believe "Black Diamond"—found its way to my nostrils. The immediate effect on my system was to make me momentarily lightheaded.

Looking into the dining room from the kitchen gave me the impression the room was dark. Once through the door, though, I saw a table, two chairs, the room in shadows, and the food for the dinner all placed on the table. At each side of the table stood a candelabrum, each with three candles. This was the only light in the room. As she came into the room, Linda switched off the kitchen lights. This completed the atmosphere. In a few moments, I heard the soft strains of Handel's Water Music coming from one of the corners of the room. The music and the perfume were having a softening effect on my willpower. Monday night, I was afraid of the implications of a candlelit atmosphere in a pizza parlor! Tonight, I had no idea what the implications of this Thanksgiving Day dinner could possibly be!

I went to her chair and seated her in the formal manner. I then seated myself across the table from her.

There was a glass of red wine before each of us at our place setting. We picked them up at the same time, each holding our glass in a position to make a toast.

"To your good health, and may our relationship be a long and joyous one," she toasted.

"To the master of this house and all who live therein. May the future be prosperous," I toasted back.

We touched the glasses together and sipped the wine.

She passed me the meat and said, "Your choice: ham, turkey, or both."

I took some ham and handed the plate back to her. Immediately, she passed the mashed potatoes and continued to pass things until my plate was full.

"This sure beats having a waiter serve you and interrupt the atmosphere of the dinner, doesn't it?" she asked.

"I can honestly say I have never been served by so elegant a waitress," I replied.

As I ate, I looked across the table at her. The light from the candles made the pearls sparkle, accentuating the bare skin around her neck and shoulders. The light from the candles was reflected in her blue eyes and softened the features of her face. The whitish-blond color of her hair formed a halo around her face to set it off even more. Lastly, the reddish blush of her lips only hinted of the lipstick she was wearing.

I, a salesman of some ability, have never put on such an impressive sales presentation for anyone in my whole life. Here I, a lonely man who only now after over twenty years of trying not to accept the loneliness I have felt, am dying to hold this person sitting across from me in my lonely arms. If only she had played Strauss waltzes instead of Handel's Water Music, I could have asked her to dance. Yet, I must be the gentleman I have tried to be all my life. And she is another man's wife. I have respected marriage all my life, and have always been a gentleman. And yet passion stirred within me as it has never stirred in years.

"What crops do they grow in the fields around here now?" I asked, trying to talk to distract myself.

"Probably the same ones they grew when you lived around here," she answered.

"But I was a city kid and never ventured too far from the safety of the city," I replied. "The farming here must have been reasonably profitable for the owners to have built such a nice house."

"This house is nearly one hundred years old, but I have no idea what the farmers were doing then. It was a dairy farm for many years. Now the land around the house is used to grow corn, soybeans, and grain crops. I grew up in the city too, remember? I haven't been a country girl for very long."

"From what I have seen of the house so far, I think you have done a marvelous job of restoring it. I saw some of the other houses near here, and they look very run-down."

"The reason we were able to afford the house and the land was because of the poor condition of the house and outbuildings. It was our first priority to restore the outside. We completed that several years ago. The kitchen was very workable when we got the house. We virtually lived in the kitchen for several years. A little of the pioneer spirit, you know," she said, laughing.

"I think the kitchen looks great. The mudroom is very functional. From what I can see in the candlelight, this dining room is very well restored. What do some of the other rooms look like?" I asked.

"This house was built with a formal parlor, a living room, this dining room, and a master bedroom off the dining room. The kitchen door enters the dining room. Between the dining room and the parlor is a foyer that contains the master staircase to the upper rooms. Just outside the mudroom is another staircase that leads up to the servant's quarters," she explained.

"Yes," I said. "Farming back then must have been very profitable."

"I have completed restoring the master bedroom in a modern style, having built in closet space and a full bathroom. Mark chose the living room and built into it closet space and a full bathroom. The parlor is useable in the summer; however, it is not heated during the winter, as it is not restored and properly insulated yet," she said.

We continued eating as she explained about the house. She told about the servant's quarters and some of the hiding places she found in the baseboards and floorboards where the young servant girls had hidden diaries and notes. These things are now part of the Edgerton History Exhibit at the library.

We ate in silence for a while. I began to think about the changes they had made to the house. Her bedroom had been the master bedroom and she made it as she wanted it to be. His bedroom was the old living room, and he had redone it as he liked. She was doing the restoration of the inside of the house. They had done the outside first. Something here was strange. Most of my married friends my age always take pains to sleep together. Some I know of will not even go to bed unless the other comes also. But there were many strange things here that I found surprising.

When the formal meal was done, she had me sit in a captain's chair in one corner of the room while she efficiently cleared the table, carrying the food and plates into the kitchen. She then placed the two candelabra on side tables in front of mirrors to reflect more light to the center of the room and pushed the dining table into a place against one wall where it looked like it belonged. The dinner chairs were placed similarly in open spots where they appeared to also belong. The center of the room now had no furniture in it. I noticed the light from the candles reflected off the polished oak flooring. She went into her bedroom for a moment and the music changed to, of all things, Strauss waltzes. I got up from my chair and started to walk toward the center of the room when she gracefully walked up before me.

"Your name is on my dance card for all evening," she said as she curtseyed.

"Then may I have this dance?" I responded.

"I am at your command," she answered.

I took her hand in mine and placed my other hand at the small of her back in the dancing position, as I had desired to do earlier during dinner. She moved closer to me. As we waltzed, her perfume again worked its magic. The softness of her body next to mine sent shivers of excitement through my body in ways I thought were lost forever.

We spoke no words; they would have been meaningless. In the shadows cast by the candles, I looked down at her face, and our eyes were drawn together. We looked deep into each other's eyes for a long moment; then she closed hers, and as we danced, she squeezed me tighter and tighter to her. The softness of her body began to engulf me to the point that when the particular waltz we were hearing was completed, I changed the way I held her. I stepped away and took her by the hand.

"I think we should sit this dance out," I said.

I was not wearing heavy clothes, and the room was not overly warm, and yet here I was sweating. My palms were sweating. What must she think? Then again, maybe hers were sweating also. I led her over to a place along the wall where two dinner chairs were close to each other, and she sat down. I pulled the other chair closer beside hers and sat down also. We sat in silence for a moment.

"May I get you a cup of punch?" I asked.

She turned and looked at me with a quizzical look.

I continued. "Over there, the punch bowl by the wall, the one with the carved ice swan in it."

At that last part of the comment, she turned to me as I looked at her, and we both began to laugh.

"Let me do better than that. I will go to the kitchen and pour us each another glass of the dinner wine," she said as she got up from her chair and headed toward the kitchen.

As I sat there, I thought back to my youth. I never went to any formal high school dances because of my injuries. I always heard that some parents forbid their children to ballroom dance. I also heard that teachers acting as chaperones at the dances required the dancers to have a certain distance between various parts of their anatomies while dancing. Until now, I didn't understand why. I had never danced that close before. When I was married, my wife and I never danced at all. Now that I think of it, that could have been part of our problem.

"Here, sir, is a glass of the finest house wine chilled to perfection," she said as she carried the two glasses of wine into the room and offered me one. She sat down beside me, and we each sipped the wine. As we sat there, the music came to an end.

I looked at the candles and said, "The candles are burning rather low, and the night is becoming late. I fear the striking of midnight, for surely I shall turn into a beast." The beast I was referring to would be found in some obscure fairy-tale. The beast I feared was found inside of me.

At that, she went to the wall and stopped the large-faced, old-fashioned regulator pendulum clock. "Now it can't strike 12:00, so you don't have to go. Besides, by now, I should have fed you enough wine to make it illegal for you to drive, and heaven knows I am in no condition to drive you home!"

Have you ever had a night that you hoped would never end, a night that could go on forever and ever without changing, repeating, or becoming boring? That was tonight. But, alas, as we sat there, she and I, each sipping our wine in silence for a minute or two, I knew this night had to end.

"I have so many memories from the years we were friends," I said.

"I think they were my happiest times," she responded.

"They were times of innocence and trust."

"And times of learning and change," she added.

"I loved you as completely as any person could, but it was not a sexual love; it was more a complete presence," I suggested.

"But my feelings were changing and I had fantasies...of you and me being together, growing together...I don't know," she said with a sigh.

"I was changing too. I was growing a beard—not much of one, but a beard anyway. I had you so high on a pedestal that I felt inadequate to reach you."

"But was my self-confidence any better?"

"I couldn't tell, but mine was misplaced. I wanted to do feats of bravery and daring to impress you and gain your admiration. Maybe I wanted to become taller to reach that pedestal on which I had placed you," I confessed.

"You were my white knight. Why didn't you realize that white knights on white horses sit higher than any statue on a pedestal?"

"I guess for me to know that I would have had to have been told. We guys seldom know these things until later. It was not that I was shy—not in general—but with you, the proper words would not come. Maybe it was a fear of rejection. Possibly I lost my nerve, or even became too embarrassed to speak around you. It could have been my looking for some sign of admiration or acceptance. That searching might have been what made me try to impress you with feats of daring. I know now that those actions were childish, but I was a child.

"During the lonely times when I am in the deer stand and nothing is happening, I think back to those days when we did things together. Those days were much simpler, and they bring forth warm memories," I said, changing the subject.

"I haven't thought about those times in years," she replied.

"Remember when we sat together the first time at the Rialto for the Saturday afternoon movies?" I asked. "How you..."

We began to talk about those days and relive some of the old memories. They were too many to recount and too long ago to matter, but we talked far into the night, even past midnight, and I didn't turn into a beast.

As the candles burned down to nothing and one by one began going out, I got up off my chair, stood, and turned toward her. "It's real late, and I must get up early and hunt tomorrow. Riley and the orange vests will all be there, and I don't want to look any more like a wimp than I already do. I better be there. If I have to, I will tie myself to the tree the stand leans against and sleep!" I said.

"And that's not wimpy?" she responded.

"Actually, it seems very acceptable; one orange vest did that this afternoon. He even got a deer," I answered. I extended my hands to her to help her up from her chair. "This has been a wonderful evening, but I really *must* go!"

"Your hunting clothes are here. You could spend the night," she proclaimed.

"That is the best offer I have had in years, and I would like to take you up on it, but we both know we would never get any sleep; we would talk all night. No! I must go," I pleaded.

She placed her arms around my neck and looked up into my face. "I love you," she said. "I always have, even when you were lost to me. Please stay." The last candle went out, and the house was as dark as it would get that night.

I looked down where she stood so tight against me and looked again at the dark form. "I love you too," I said as I tightened my arms around her and gave her a long, tight hug.

She gave a sigh and snuggled in. We held that position for some time. I knew the time had come for me to leave. I untangled my arms from her, as she did hers from me. In the dark, I turned to head for the kitchen and the door. I found my clothes bundle and was beginning to open the door to leave.

"Can I see you tomorrow night?" she asked. "I can't have you so close and not see you!"

I made no reply to her question. I couldn't trust myself to say the honorable thing. I stood there mute, me, a salesman who never ran out of words; this was becoming a habit. I walked out of the door, into the cold, dark night, heading across the porch toward the steps and walkway leading to my car.

"I will be at your motel at 6:30 tomorrow night." She spoke loudly to make sure I heard. Her voice echoed from the farm buildings in the yard as she stood there in the darkened door of her house.

I returned to Janesville without further incident, parked the car, and entered the lobby.

"You still getting up at 5:30 to go hunting tomorrow?" the desk clerk asked.

"That's what I came up here to do, so I will be out teasing the deer tomorrow morning." I tried to sound upbeat as I spoke.

"You'd be better off sitting down here talking to me than trying to get such little sleep," he said.

"Just call me at the proper time," I answered, and headed up to the room.

A Wounded Lady

It is late Friday night, and I am back in the motel room again. In some respects, I don't really know what I am doing here or why I have even stayed tonight. A word to the wise, though: if any of you want to get your deer and you are hunting in the rain, falling snow, and very cold weather, make sure to keep your shotgun well oiled. Today, I found out Wisconsin deer are not spooked by WD-40.

The telephone rang at 5:30, but instead of the normal music from the automatic system, it was the wild and woolly infinitely bored desk clerk kidding me about sleeping in and chiding me for being such a slovenly deer hunter. Most salesmen can tolerate wiseguys because we understand them. Generally, we are considered in some circles to *be* wiseguys. At 5:30 a.m., after maybe two and one-half hours of a fitful sleep, a wiseguy desk clerk could only be thankful he was not strangled, stabbed, or shot to death.

I sat up on the edge of the bed. I hadn't had that much wine, so why did my head hurt? My mouth tasted like I had been chewing on a decaying mouse. The frantic acid in my stomach not only wanted to eat its way out, it wanted to escape from the top, too. My eyes were bleary, my muscles stiff, and my throat sore from sinus drainage. And I wanted to go and kill a deer? I felt as though the deer had somehow gotten revenge on me!

I dressed fast. The heck with washing! No deer was going to look behind my ears anyway. My sole objective was to get out of the room, into the Sable, and out on my stand without either dying from sleep deprivation or an accidental gunshot wound of my own.

The details of how I got to the stand are still hazy. I remember the quick stop and two bottles of coke. I have no idea what I ate. I had to close one eye to drive the Sable because I couldn't focus on anything in the dark with both open. I opened the windows so the twenty-degree air could shock my face and body. I closed the windows because I couldn't drive in a straight line shivering and shaking as badly as I was. It could be compared to a man dying of thirst doing anything to get the relief of water. In my case, I was dying to get up on the stand and go to sleep.

I arrived at the stand and somehow managed to move myself, my gun, and the rope to tie me to the stand up to the top. I loaded my gun and tied it to the ladder. I tied myself to the tree with the rope around my chest as I had seen the orange vest do. I nodded backward with my head.

The next thing I remember is hanging with my arms and head over one side of the stand and my feet over the other with the barrel of my gun kind of poking me in the stomach. Well, the safety worked; I didn't get shot. I looked around and hadn't seen any orange vests yet. They either saw me and were lying on the ground too weak from laughter to get up, or they hadn't arrived yet.

Having shocked my adrenaline into action with my last maneuver, I sat at the top of the stand, organized myself again, and waited for the hands of my little watch to show 9:00 a.m. I wanted dearly to go back to the motel and sleep. Moral of the story: you just don't put an old man on the top of a stand after he has had two hours of sleep—a young man, yes; an old man, *no.*

The sun rose on another cloud-covered day, and I dozed very carefully. Then, all of a sudden, to my right, up the hill where the orange vest had shot the small buck, I heard a shot. I looked over my shoulder and saw a deer coming my way. Then, smelling something—probably my failure to clean up this morning—he headed over toward the woods behind me. Somebody took a shot that came zinging at the ground safely to the right of me. The deer continued toward the woods to my left and stopped. Something there spooked him.

A number of shots rang out, confusing the deer, causing him to come in my direction. I reached for my gun. I put it to my shoulder, tried to push the safety, and nothing happened! It would not move! Apparently, my rapid motion spooked him, as he turned back toward the woods. Another fusillade of shotgun fire convinced him that my direction was safer. I was still trying to get my safety unstuck as he was coming toward me. I had thrown my gloves to the ground when he was heading away from me, and I was still trying to get the sliding shaft of the safety, located in the trigger guard ahead of the trigger, to move. Somehow, whether from the heat of my hands melting the ice holding it while I tried to loosen it or the force of my adrenaline acting—I will never know—something happened. The deer was coming at me. I was concentrating on getting the safety loose so I could aim my gun and fire. The safety came loose. My finger slipped, pulling the trigger. The gun discharged. The recoil from the firing almost knocked me off the stand. The deer instinctively ducked from the sound and by doing so ended up right in the path of the slug. It fell over dead on the spot. I recovered my gun and my composure before I noticed the deer was mine.

Riley and the orange vests came out of the woods to look at the deer and congratulate me on the cool way I handled the situation: not firing, but waiting until I had that one-in-a-million shot, how I had anticipated the motion of the deer and shot into it. The praise continued as I gutted the deer. I even got the guts out without puncturing the bladder. They told me how John had messed up his first deer so they couldn't even eat the meat. Each told how if they had my patience it would have been their deer, and they all congratulated me again on what a fine hunter I was. If they only knew!

In the beginning, they said, they had wondered why John had asked such an inept hunter to come and hunt with him. They took bets on which day I would shoot myself. The day I put up my tent, they wondered if I knew which end of the gun to shoot with. Today, they had their answers. Some of us survive on sheer luck!

"Riley," I said as I was finishing gutting the deer and placing the preliminary tag, "I have my buck and really can't hunt anymore this season. One of your fellows is free to take over the stand."

"Mighty fine of you to offer."

I cut out the tenderloins and packed them in snow inside the carcass to chill them and keep them from drying out. I got out my rope, tied it to the rack, and dragged the deer though the hole in the fence. I retrieved my tarp from the bottom of the ladder and headed to the Sable. I got the deer loaded on the hood. It was too large to fit on the small trunk deck on the back of the car. I drove the deer into Edgerton to register it. I also made arrangements with a local person to butcher the carcass and mount the head for me. This took the rest of the morning and lasted well into the afternoon.

When I first got to town, I thought I could get this all taken care of and fly home to Atlanta tonight. I thought about stopping at the library and saying a fast good-bye to Linda and being done with it. Things rarely go as planned, though, when you are in unfamiliar surroundings.

I realized when I got to the motel I also had some cleaning that had to be done. It was apparent the bloody clothes had to be washed before I could take them home. I remembered I had seen a coin laundry in Janesville and I went to wash the blood from the hunting clothes. I decided there would be time to shower later, so I went directly from the motel to the coin laundry.

By the time the well-insulated clothes were clean and dried, I had been in the laundry dozing for several hours. That naptime rejuvenated me quite well. I got back to the motel exactly at 6:30, in time to see Linda walk through the lobby doors and go to the desk to call my room. I grabbed my bundle of clothes and reached the desk just as the desk clerk was telling her I was not answering the phone.

"Hi!" she said as she came up to me and placed her arm through the crook of the elbow of the arm carrying the washed clothing.

"Hi," I said back to her.

She continued to walk with me as I headed to the elevator on my way to my room. I didn't invite her to my room. She was inviting herself.

I didn't want her there while I changed, but I didn't really know how to tell her to stay in the lobby either. Again, a salesman without words! Will I ever be able to sell again?

We got to the door, and she took the little card and opened the door for me. She followed me into the room. It was dark in there when she closed the door. Before I could turn on a light switch, I smelled her perfume coming toward me; then her arms were around my neck in what could be called a lovelock, and her lips met mine. I could feel the heat of her body as she pressed against me, and I felt the special sensations it caused. It was too late; all I could think to do was to drop my washed clothes, kiss her, and hug her tight. I liked the shivers that were going through my body. I liked the feeling I had of her giving of herself unfettered, unconditionally, and completely. No woman had ever come upon me like that before—not even my wife!

As we hugged and kissed, we moved a little in the room and somehow bumped into the king-sized bed. With her weight against me, I more or less fell onto the bed with her on top of me. I feared I might have hurt her, but she seemed to be fine as she slid herself more toward my head so she could kiss me with more force.

Her weight and her deep kissing were beginning to affect my ability to breathe, so I gently rolled with her so we were each lying on our sides facing each other on the bed. She kissed me, she rubbed against me, and then she kissed some more. I kissed back, and I didn't want to stop, but eventually I knew this just could not continue to go on like this. I rolled over and hit the light switch on the wall light. The sudden glare caused her to close her eyes for a moment. I kissed each closed eye in turn and continued to hug her. By the time shown on the clock, we must have been at this for half an hour.

"Linda," I said, "I really should get showered and shaved so I can look presentable when we go to eat."

"Who said anything about eating?"

"I ate well last night, and now my stomach wants to have a rematch with more food," I joked. "And I also have the tenderloins from today's deer for you to cook and eat before your husband comes home."

"They called," she said. "They haven't seen a deer yet this whole trip. They think the snow is too deep. I heard about your deer."

"If you only knew the truth," I said laughingly.

"I overslept this morning—I don't know why—so I didn't pack a lunch. I decided I would go home and snack at noon. I started to drive out 106 and ended up stopping at the truck stop at I-90. I overheard them talking about your deer," she said.

"You can't believe everything you hear," I commented. "By the way, what did you hear?"

"There were several hunters eating and talking about how professionally you shot the deer. You waited for the last minute for the perfect shot, you did not rush it, and then you shot where he ducked for a perfect kill. They were impressed!"

"It was a lucky shot, one in a million," I answered. "Probably never happen again."

"Well, you sure made believers out of them," came her reply.

I am dense, but sometimes things have a way of getting through to me anyhow. Was she impressed by my kill? Did hearing the orange vests at the truck stop restaurant elevate me to the level of brave and daring? Was I the caveman bringing home the bacon and getting the prettiest girl? Had I inadvertently done here what I failed to do on a motorcycle forty years ago? Was my ego getting fluffed and puffed here?

I had planned on telling her how it happened, the suicidal deer wandering into the path of my accidentally discharged slug. But now I decided that I had better let well enough alone.

"Would you like to freshen up and go to the lobby while I clean up and change?" I asked her.

"Why?" she asked. "We are both adults, and I won't be embarrassed. After all, I raised three sons. It isn't as if I haven't ever seen a man naked or in underwear before."

"I guess if you want to stay, don't say I didn't warn you," I responded.

My wife was a nurse, and she, in the early days, could not look at my burned area without leaving the room. It was never a pretty sight. We had to make love in the dark because of it. I guess on anyone else she probably could have taken the medical aloofness that goes with the job and accepted it. I guess that maybe I was too close to her for her to do that. Later, after she left and I tried to become intimate with other women, they always wanted to see the area. That was the last I saw of them. In any case, I could take enough clothing in the bathroom with me so I would not be embarrassed.

Still under the influence of about a half hour of kissing and heavy petting, I went into the bathroom and closed the door. I took my clothes off and placed them on the sink area. I turned on the water and adjusted the temperature of the shower so it was nice and warm. I stepped into the bathtub and pulled the shower curtain closed. What I really needed was a cold shower. I wet my head and began to shampoo my hair when I felt a disturbance in the air around me. My hair was full of shampoo that was threatening to get into my eyes, so I didn't see her. The sound of the water around my ears blanked out any noise she made. Suddenly, I was startled by her hand on my back. I am not one to scream when startled like that, but I sort of jumped, knocking my head on the shower nozzle. I let out a yell as the pain shot through my scalp. This startled her, causing her to scream and lose her footing on the slippery porcelain of the tub behind me. When you consider we were both fifty-six years old and slightly overweight, we wouldn't be that agile standing in the tub. My eyes were beginning to burn as the shampoo began to work its way into them. I didn't see her slide down the wall at the back of the tub toward me. She had to be about halfway down when she knocked my feet from under me and I began to fall. Instinctively, knowing she must now be under me, I tried to throw myself to one side so as to not hurt her. The maneuver somewhat worked, as I slid down the shower wall somewhat on and somewhat beside her.

Her screaming had stopped. My eyes were still closed and burning. I was too far from the spraying water to clear the shampoo. I wanted to reach for the towel, but all I could feel was her body next to mine in the tub. She wasn't speaking or laughing or generally making any noise, so I moved as fast as I could to get at a towel and wipe the soap from my eyes. I pulled the shower curtain away and found her dazed in the bottom of the tub, having apparently hit her head on the way down. She half sat and half lay in the bottom of the tub, shaking her head as if to clear it. It looked like there was some blood in her hair.

I tried to talk to her. "Are you okay?"

Finally, she got her senses back enough to answer. "I think...I...am okay, but, but I have this terrible headache." She answered in a hesitating manner. She shook her head as she answered, and I saw blood running rather quickly from the hair on her head down the wall and onto the white porcelain of the tub.

"Do you think you can get out of the shower, or should we call for the medics to come and take you to the emergency room?" I asked.

"I don't want the emergency medics here!" she answered. "Could you turn off the water?"

I looked at her and saw the blood running down her back and on her shoulders. That was a good point; in all of the confusion and concern for her as she lay there, I had totally forgotten to turn off the shower.

I looked at her and smiled. "Good point," I said as I reached into the tub and turned the water off. "Now do you want to get out of the tub?"

"In just a minute," she answered as she moved around in the tub, making the bump on her head visible to me. I could see a gash about three-fourths of an inch long that was bleeding fast.

"Let me check that bump." I got a wet washcloth from the sink and tried to stop the flow of blood.

She leaned her head toward me, and I pulled her hair aside to get a better view. "Ouch! That hurt!" she said as I pressed the washcloth near the bump.

The bump looked like a golf ball that had been cut by a club, large, round and bulging about an eighth of an inch up from the back of her head with this bleeding gash in it.

She was still naked, so I gave her a towel to cover with while I wiped the blood from her back and hair. I extended my hand to help her out of the tub. She held the towel in front with one hand as she used my other hand to steady herself. I tried to keep the cold washcloth compressed on her cut. She carefully got out of the tub. I helped her balance by holding one arm as I walked her to the bed. She lay down.

"Thank you!" she said as I elevated her feet with the pillows from the head of the bed.

"I have to rinse off," I stated. "Then we will both dress and I will take you to the emergency room at Mercy hospital and get you looked at. That is a nasty bump."

"I'm okay!" she said emphatically.

"I believe you think you are, but I want to be sure!" I got back in the shower to rinse off.

I dried and rapidly dressed, trying to lose no time getting her to the emergency room at the hospital. I helped her dry off and dress, and we both got bundled up to go. The blood was still coming out from the gash in the back of her head. She took a scarf from her purse and tried to stop the blood with that. Even with the scarf, she still got blood down the back of her coat. I walked slowly with her to the doors of the motel. I had her wait while I got the Sable. Even I was a little wobbly from the effects of my fall in the tub as I walked through icy ruts of parking lot. I walked more stiffly and more carefully to the car. When I parked the Sable near the motel door, I got out of the car and came to where she was standing. It would do no good to have her fall again! I helped her get into the Sable to make sure she didn't fall. I tried to shield the back of the seat from as much of the seeping blood as possible. The bleeding had slowed, and Linda held the scarf very tight, trying to control the flow. By the time we had gotten into the car, though, her hair was all bloody, and the back of her coat was a mess.

I drove to Mercy hospital as fast as I could, as I didn't like the looks of the bump on her head. I believed that she had been knocked out, and I feared that she could have had some internal bleeding. I needed the best diagnosis possible to be reassured that she was okay.

I stopped at the emergency room door and helped her from the car. I walked with her until she was safely in the emergency room and helped getting her settled. I then hurried out the door, drove to the parking lot, and parked the Sable. The heavy cloud cover added dreariness to the darkness of the night, which at this time was as dark as my mood. By the time I got back to the emergency room, she was already in one of the emergency cubicles. I asked about her. The nurse said I should wait, as the lady wanted to get my name and thank me for helping her when she fell. She was probably in really good shape if she could think that far ahead to cover my bringing her in. I settled into a chair in the waiting room and waited. Sometime later, around 11:00, a nurse woke me up and gave me an update as to Linda's condition.

"She is fine, a possible very mild concussion with no internal bleeding. She has three stitches in the cut, and the bleeding has stopped. Her blood pressure has come down, and she should be able to drive her car. She has asked if you were still here. When I said you were, she asked me to ask you if you would drive her to her car so she can drive home. Will you?" the nurse asked.

"I would be glad to," I answered, and the nurse left.

In a few minutes, Linda appeared with an ice bag on her head and the nurse by her side.

"I am so glad you stopped to help me when I fell," she said. "I feel so bad about delaying you like this, but I wanted to thank you personally for your generous help. I appreciate so much you agreeing to drive me back to my car. What is your name?"

"I am Peter Woods," I answered. I tried to use a name that would not be recognized, but all I could think of at the spur of the moment was Woods. After all, the name, when translated into German, has wood in it. "And you are?"

"Just call me Linda," she answered. "It is so good to have met you."

"I will get the car and pick you up here if that is okay," I said.

"That will be fine," she answered. "Let me take care of the emergency room charges, and I will meet you outside."

Once in the car, knowing that she was okay, I relaxed a little. "I will drive you home," I said, taking charge.

"I guess that will be okay. I am so sorry this had to happen," she said apologetically.

"I am, too," I responded sadly. "What were you doing in there with me anyhow? What were you thinking?"

"I wanted to surprise you and wash your back and then have you do mine. It has been years since I showered with a man, and it just felt like the thing to do," she answered. "Besides, I just felt girlish, and I wanted to do something daring and exciting!"

"It sure would have been," I answered. "I think it would have been different at least; but it was, in fact, very exciting in a much different way."

"Were you worried about me? I really would not have had to go to the emergency room. I thought I was okay," she said.

"Tonight, I found out I care for you—not that the thought had not crossed my mind before. It was just seeing you hurt and bleeding that brought what I have suppressed to the surface, where I guess it will stay. I will come and get you tomorrow morning when you feel better so you can get your car. Then I think it would be best for me to drive to Chicago, turn in the rental car, and fly home to Atlanta. That should uncomplicate your life. I wish it could be otherwise, but reality is what it is."

She was silent for a time. "Will you stay until Sunday night? I know you have your deer and will not be hunting anymore. Could you spend the last two days with me?" She reached over and lifted the armrests for the front seats to the up position and cuddled as close to me as the seatbelt would allow.

There was a long silence as we drove north on I-90 and took the 106 exit. Finally, as we neared her house, I had to answer her. I had mulled that over and over in my mind, and, finally, I responded with a question. "My being here will only make the parting that much more painful, will it not?"

"True, but the memories will never be lost. Anyway, there may be an answer for us within the next two days. Please stay. Tomorrow, I want to have you for the whole day!" she demanded as she reached over and kissed me on the cheek and blew in my ear.

The shivers I was becoming so used to were back again.

When we reached her house, I walked her up the porch steps and across the porch to her kitchen door. I took her in my arms. My goodnight kiss was long and tender, and the feeling of her against me, even through all the clothes one wears on a cold Wisconsin night, was warm and comforting.

"Good night," was all I could think to say as I turned and walked across the porch and down the steps toward the Sable.

The cold snow on the driveway made that funny crunching sound as I walked along. I got in the car, started it, and waved good-bye to the figure standing in the door waving back as I drove off.

I did a lot of thinking on my drive back to Janesville. *Here is this lost friend from the past. Could I call her a lost love? I don't know how to answer that one. At the time we were friends, it definitely was a case of deep like, yet was that love? Yet, at that age and at that time, we were so close that the idea of romantic love was somewhat assumed. I definitely did not act toward her as though she were my sister. In many respects, I tried to win her love. On the other hand, she had those fantasies that could have been considered love.*

Times were so simple! Was she trying to create a romantic interlude in the shower, or was she trying to live a youthful fantasy? At our age! Yet we were both acting very young just minutes before. What would a couple of young persons the age of her children have thought had they seen that? Would they have seen a couple of old people acting in a manner that would have been disgusting to them? I wonder. When I was fourteen, I would have bet anyone that my parents didn't have sex. They seemed too old! And tonight the two of us were acting so strange for a couple old enough to be grandparents!

How to assess this? How can one make sense of it? It, in many respects, can be looked at from a distance. There is a lot happening, and all I can do is watch. I am already wounded. Why am I here? Why did I stay?

When I got back to the motel and went to the room, I found it was a mess. It took a long time to clean up all the blood. I even went out to the Sable and washed down the passenger seat.

A Day in Milwaukee

It is Saturday night, or actually early Sunday morning. I am back in the Janesville motel room. I am getting ready to go to sleep.

Today started when I got out of bed without the alarm. I took a hot, leisurely shower that seemed to relax some of the soreness from last night's fall in the tub. I got dressed in what I had packed as my traveling clothes: white shirt, gray pullover sweater, gray slacks, black socks, and loafers. I wore my Atlanta winter car coat, which was a little light for the cold weather up here, but I didn't expect to be out in the weather that much today anyway. I left the motel room for the lobby at 9:00.

When I got to the lobby, the friendly desk clerk had his wisecrack of the day all ready. "The way you are dressed you must be on your way to socialize with the deer! You are definitely not dressed to hunt them."

This was said by the guy who told me I had to talk Norwegian to the deer to attract them.

"My deer is being processed by someone in Edgerton. I just decided to pursue some of the finer things Janesville has to offer, such as sitting by the bank of the frozen Rock River and watching the water flow," I answered.

"If that is exciting," he responded, "you should go by and watch the water tower drip."

"I tried that, but those large icicles make that much too dangerous a hobby," I countered.

"Just because you Southerners never learned to duck icicles doesn't mean the sport is dangerous to us. How do you think we keep the population of Southerners so low?" he said jokingly.

Now I had him! "One day below twenty degrees is enough to prove to any good Southerner that it makes no sense whatsoever to live up here," I answered. With that, I headed for the door and the Sable.

The effect of the bright sunshine hit as soon as I stepped out the door. I had been so used to the overcast and cloudy weather we had been having that my eyes were shocked by the brightness of the day. The sun reflecting from the white snow was so bright I had to close one eye and squint with the other just to see. A beautiful day can definitely lift one's spirits, and this sunny day seemed destined to do that. The slight tinting on the windows of the Sable helped me acclimate my eyes to the sunshine, and as I looked around, everything appeared bright and fresh.

I followed my usual routine, only several hours later than usual. I went to the quick stop and bought my coffee and sweet roll. I got back in the Sable and headed onto the road, only this time I turned to go up the on ramp of I-90 North. I was on my way to spend the day with Linda. That, along with the beauty of the day, worked to keep my spirits high. I felt the excitement of going to some unknown, new adventure. Whatever Linda did would be a surprise. After what happened last night, she was the total unknown.

As I drove, my mind went back to other aspects of last night that had not really surfaced until I was wide-awake this morning. Here I was in a room with a naked lady, and yet I had not paid much attention to the fact. She had come into the shower naked, and at the time, that would have been in the context of romance. This would have excited me and led me to other romantic acts. When she became hurt, one of the first reflexes was to offer her the towel that she modestly used to cover herself. Had she used it to give warmth, she would have draped it differently.

When I was a youth, just the thought of a nude woman would excite me. Even one in a tight swimsuit would get my lingering attention. The whole female body was an exotic mystery. One of the most exciting things I remember doing was looking at the lingerie section of the Sears Roebuck catalog. This was like reading a road map showing places to visit someday. I could spend a lot of time digesting the various forms of the models. Later, after the accident, when I was in the hospitals recovering, I was attracted to the younger nurses, but it was never led to anything, but the most professional relationship. How do you date in a hospital anyway? If there had been a way, I would have found it; of that I am sure. There were no long lines of girls waiting to talk to me on Sunday afternoons.

Mothers are great, but mothers are mothers, and they have no idea what a young son wants. I had my pictures of favorite movie stars in bathing suits. I guess you could have called them my pin-up girls. That was as close as I got to girlfriends. There was a time when we still lived in Edgerton, before I was released from the hospital, when I dreamed of trying to win Linda. Those dreams vanished when the reality hit that Linda was not visiting me.

John handled my questions very diplomatically, but eventually I came to the conclusion I was damaged goods and not the white knight in shining armor dateable girls looked for.

When we moved to Detroit, my reputation stayed in Edgerton. My physical looks came with me. The least of my problems was the lift I had to wear on my right shoe. I was a bit clumsy, but that was almost able to be hidden by only raising the heel. It was the burn scarring yet to be fixed on a part of my face that seemed to shock people. I could see it in their eyes. The attempt to look away the first time they met me, the other little motions of their head. I had a lot of friends that were girls, but never any that would get close enough for me to consider them girlfriends. So my appearance was a detriment, and the girls were cold to me. I now realize that much of that was probably my own inability to be comfortable around them. I had not developed the innate dating skills other young men my age had. The result was predictable: I didn't date.

After the last of the plastic surgeries that cleaned up my face, attitudes changed. I probably exuded more self-confidence. I no longer saw the girls' eyes look away from me, and their heads didn't move in the old way. The change was dramatic. And then came Milwaukee, and Jennifer.

While I had been driving deep in thought, the time and the miles had passed. I was now heading up the road to Linda's house. I had never seen the house and buildings in daylight before. The house looked very majestic in the bright sunlight. The shingles on the roof appeared to be black, with tints of gray. The eaves were somewhat plain, with just a little scrollwork around each of the corners. The siding on the house was what might have been referred to as clapboard siding years ago. It was painted white and gave a good appearance to the house. The upper windows were close to the eaves but had decorative wood trim on each side and below the sill. The lower windows had a decorative cornice at the top and the decorative wood trim on the sides and below the sill.

The front and side porches were designed with posts that stood from the porch floor to support the roof. At the top of each post was scrollwork that added that touch of class. The posts were square for about a foot at the top and about three feet at the bottom. The area between the squared portions was circular with grooves and shapes turned into it. This made very attractive posts. Each porch had a railing between the posts that was made up of small, decorative posts that extended to the floor. That house design was always somewhat plain, but the little trim pieces tended to accent it enough so it didn't look like a bunch of boxes pushed together. At the foundation was snow-covered shrubbery.

The rows of evergreen trees that formed the wind break on the north and west sides of the house were a pleasant contrast to the white of the house and the snow on the ground.

The rest of the farm buildings consisted of a barn and what looked like a tool shed. Both were painted red and accented with white trim. The shade trees that surrounded the house and the other buildings seemed to be hardwoods and looked rather naked standing in the snow. The overall effect as I drove closer was to remind me of the many Currier and Ives prints of winter scenes I had seen throughout my life. It certainly was a peaceful setting in which to live.

I drove the car into the driveway and parked so that we could get in easily without stepping in the plowed snow along the side of the driveway. I walked to the porch, up the steps, and across to the door. As I was about to knock, Linda opened the door.

She looked very beautiful standing in that open door. "Hi!" she said and smiled at me.

"How do you feel?" I asked, smiling back. That was probably the dumbest thing I could have said, but her beauty was overwhelming, and anything else I might have said would have probably sounded just as dumb. Her hair was done in the usual way. She was wearing a white blouse under a tight red pullover sweater that showed her good figure. She was wearing black, tailored, wool slacks. She had some kind of fleece-lined indoor/outdoor high-topped boots on her feet.

"I feel great," she answered. "I'm ready for a day of fun and excitement. I packed a lunch of Thanksgiving Day leftovers and am ready for you to show me the world."

Obviously, my original plan of taking her back to get her car was not even viable now. By the time we had her car back here, it would be noon, and she would be in no mood to eat a romantic lunch here. Plan A was dead. Now to come up with plan B. Chicago would be all crowded with Christmas shoppers. Milwaukee was close, so Milwaukee it was.

"Get your coat and scarf," I commanded. "Give me the picnic basket, and we will be on our way."

"Where are we going?" she asked. She had put on a dark blue, long overcoat with a collar that could be raised to give her head some protection from the wind. Her scarf was blue plaid, broad-woven wool that, when tied at the neck, covered about three-quarters of her head. When she tied it, I could see the rise in the fabric over the bump on her head.

"To show you the world, my dear!" I replied as I opened the door and helped her into the Sable. I got in and started the engine. Instantly, we had heat. I drove to 106, turned north to pick up the 26 bypass at Fort Atkinson, and headed through Jefferson to Johnson's Creek. I stopped and filled the Sable with fuel before entering the on-ramp to I-94 East.

We were on our way. The adventure had begun. I only had a faint idea of what I wanted to do, but Milwaukee has many interesting places to visit, and it had been a long time since I had been back to many of them.

We continued to drive east on I-94, admiring the snow-covered farm fields and the various natural wonders. Coming over the hill and looking at the Nashotah Lakes was probably the prettiest view of the trip so far. The last time we came by here was Tuesday night, and the view was not that good, considering the falling snow and all. As we continued to drive toward Milwaukee, I decided we would eat our lunch at one of the parking places overlooking Lake Michigan. I remembered a parking lot off Lake Shore Drive next to the public beach, and if the snow was plowed and it was clear, we could park there. It jutted out slightly into the lake and had water on almost three sides. I decided it would be the perfect place to eat the picnic lunch Linda had so thoughtfully prepared.

As we continued to drive, Linda asked about my parents and how they stood the change when they moved to Detroit. I asked her about her parents and what had happened to them. She told me about how it was to raise her three boys and the special things they had done as children. We talked about the changes that had taken place around Edgerton, such as the old school buildings having been renovated to serve the very people who had been taught there so long ago. It was the kind of small talk that old friends do when they are catching up on old gossip or, in this case, history.

She told me about some interesting things she had found in the servants' quarters of her old house. I learned about the Edgerton history section in the old library. I hadn't known it, but Edgerton even has a small museum of tobacco history hidden away in one of the downtown buildings.

I learned the Carlton Hotel had been purchased and renovated by someone from out of town and was going to be put back into use as a bar and hotel to attract the well heeled students of historical experience. The renovation had been well done and looked good. Then something happened, either in the electrical wiring or some part of the heating system, and it caught fire. There was nothing left to save, so it turned to ash and became a parking lot.

The Rialto had long outlived its commercial usefulness and, having been damaged by the fire, had to be torn down. Most of the yellow-brick tobacco warehouses on West Fulton Street were brought down by fire or the desire of the townsfolk to clean up that side of the street. The railroad depot had been restored most of the way now, and would become something useful.

On and on about the town relics, she talked. It was good to hear her voice, and I appreciated the knowledge, but for the most part, it was history only of interest to those who lived there.

We drove into Milwaukee on I-94 past the State Fair Park in West Allis. We continued past the Milwaukee County Stadium, home of the Milwaukee Braves when I lived in Milwaukee. When Jennifer and I moved to Atlanta, the Braves followed a short time later. The stadium was now the home of the Brewers, an American League club. The stadium was being replaced by a new one, and things had changed.

As we continued, we saw three very tall conical bulges to our right. These looked very strange protruding through the snow. I told Linda we would explore those later. We continued inbound toward the lakefront. It was hard to imagine that she had lived so close for so many years and had never explored the wonders of Milwaukee.

We found the parking lot I had remembered, and it was indeed plowed. Lake Michigan reminded me of the Gulf of Mexico, or even the Atlantic Ocean, as I looked at the great expanse of water. The big difference was that the waves were smaller. The sun shone on the water, making it look inviting, yet the very angle of the sun reminded me that winter was approaching and it was cold outside. As we sat there eating the picnic lunch in the twenty-degree weather, I was thankful for the meal and the fact the Sable had a good heater.

"Did you ever sit by Lake Michigan when you visited Chicago?" I asked.

"We drove by it many times, but we never stopped," she replied.

"This was a great place to come and have a picnic. I remember the hot days in August, when the rest of Milwaukee was sweltering, we would come down here and eat supper over at picnic tables placed on the grass."

I pointed to the pile of plowed snow covering the grassy area over to the left.

"The sun would be setting behind the buildings up on the cliff, and a cool lake breeze would come in and make it very pleasant. I guess we lost that when we moved to Atlanta," I mused.

"That was with Jennifer?" Linda asked.

"Yeah," I answered. "I guess I was thinking back to a simpler time."

"You still miss her?" Linda asked.

Now we were trampling on some sacred ground. Did I miss her? I guess after all these years I missed the companionship. How could I answer that question?

"I don't believe I miss her. I hold nothing against her. I sincerely hope she is happy," I replied. "You know, when I first saw the Atlantic Ocean down on Tybee Island in Georgia, I said it reminded me of Lake Michigan. Jennifer was with me then. To answer your question, I don't miss Jennifer; I just feel a loneliness for someone."

Linda moved closer, gently leaning her shoulder against mine. We ate in silence while we watched the waves roll onto shore, splash, and deposit spray that turned to ice in the sand. We watched the local birds as they flew out over the lake and back again. I have no idea what kind of birds they are anymore; they just remind me of the seagulls that live near the Atlantic coast.

When we had finished eating and became bored watching the water, Linda packed the remains of the lunch into the basket she brought and placed it in the backseat. We drove out of the parking lot south on Lakeside Drive to a most unique building: the Milwaukee Veteran's Memorial.

"Did you ever hear of the Veteran's Memorial?" I asked.

"When I was growing up, my father had wanted to drive in to visit the various museums and such in Milwaukee, but we never did. Mark has no interest in anything of an arty nature. When we went somewhere and had the choice, we went to Chicago, as it was bigger and had more things to see," she answered.

I drove into a parking lot near the Veteran's Memorial and parked the car.

"Here we are. May I give you a personal tour of the interior?" I asked. "They used to have paintings hanging on the walls."

"Kind sir, I would very much appreciate if you would," came her reply. She looked at me, and we both began to laugh.

"I doubt there will be any paintings I will remember in there," I said. "In any case, we will see what we can find. This unique structure was designed by Finnish architect Eliel Saarinen and has been here since before I came here to school. I have no idea when it was built."

We entered at lakefront level and climbed the stairs to what could be called Milwaukee street level. We then climbed to the next level and generally explored the place. There were pictures on the walls, and the place was decorated in the Christmas holiday tradition.

We got back in the car, and, again, she moved closer to me so our shoulders were touching. If she was trying to dispel the lonely feelings the lake had given me, she actually was doing a pretty good job of it. I decided she might like to see the view of Milwaukee from the new bridge that went south over the river. I was curious to see what was on the other side anyway.

I took the I-794 roadway over the bridge to the south side. We exited at Jones Island. As we drove around the harbor slips there, I recounted the ore ships Jennifer and I had seen moored here for the winter so many years ago. There were none here now. I guess they don't use many ore carriers anymore.

Milwaukee does have some ships that come to the port to load and unload foreign goods. It was very late in the season, though, so there were very few ships at the docks. There was a date for the St. Lawrence Seaway to close for the winter. If the ships here at the dock didn't get out before that date, they would be here for the winter. There was nothing happening on Jones Island, so we drove back to Wisconsin Avenue.

Wisconsin Avenue is pretty much the main street in Milwaukee, and the big department stores used to call it home. Naturally, that made it the street to decorate for Christmas. It was decorated, but these decorations seemed to pale when compared to those I remembered from when I lived there. We drove out to 35th Street, where I made a left turn and headed for the bridge.

As we approached the bridge, visible in the distance across the valley were three large, conical bumps rising from the bluff. These were the Geodesic Domes of the Milwaukee Botanical Gardens.

"I told you I would explain those to you later. Now here we are on our way to visit them," I said. "I thought it better to satisfy the hunger before satisfying the sense of smell."

She looked at me and laughed. "You do have such a way with words."

Although the domes and the park are just across the 27th Street Bridge over the Industrial Valley, the domes can best be seen from the distance while crossing the 35th Street viaduct. I crossed and drove us to the entrance. The park actually has a name. It is called the Mitchell Park Horticultural Conservatory. Who would have guessed?

"They sure look big," Linda said.

"They were finished around the time Jennifer and I got married," I told her. "We visited them a couple of times before we moved to Atlanta."

"Was coming here a bad idea?" Linda asked. "I wanted to spend this day with you alone, not with you and the ghost of Jennifer!"

"I'm sorry," I said. "There are certain things I remember about my old stomping ground, and I guess one of them happens to be Jennifer. This may have been a bad idea. If I have marred your day by mentioning her, I am sorry. For me, coming here will probably bring back enough memories to make me somewhat melancholy at night for several months. Let me drop you off here at the entrance so you won't have to walk far in the cold. I'll go park the car."

"No. Let me come with you!" she requested. "I want to hold your hand while we walk to the entrance together."

"Okay," I answered as I left the drop-off area and drove toward the parking lot.

I got out of the car and went to her side to open the door for her. She actually waited for me to do that. It was later in the day, and the sun was lower in the sky, so the chill of the Wisconsin day was penetrating my Atlanta-weight winter coat. When we got into the entrance, I checked my watch.

"Will your husband call at 6:00 tonight?"

"No," she answered. "Why did you ask?"

"I was looking at the time and estimating when we will have to leave this place to get you home to answer the phone," was my reply.

"I told him last night I probably would not be home and he shouldn't bother to call," she answered.

I decided to leave well enough alone and not answer her. I walked up to the ticket window and bought two tickets to enter the Horticultural Conservatory and went back to where I left her standing.

"Let's go in," I said.

We entered and began our walk through the domes. One dome was tropical plants, such as you would find in South America. One dome was desert-type plants. The third dome had a Christmas display in it. As we wandered through the domes, we talked about various places each of us had visited. We sat on a bench in the Christmas dome and talked about Christmases past.

I, finding the season very lonely when at home in Atlanta, had usually spent that holiday time traveling. I feel less lonely when I am in a crowd. In my work as a salesman, I have traveled throughout most of the United States, some in Canada, and a little in Mexico. I have various places where I enjoy the Christmas crowds. She had rarely traveled out of central Wisconsin and had never spent Christmas away from her family. As we talked, she seemed to like to listen to my descriptions of the places I had been and how Christmas was celebrated at each. The temperature in the dome was a little chilly, but the atmosphere created by the display was pleasant and left me with a warm feeling inside. We sat and talked there for a long time.

It was dusk when we left the domes.

"Race you to the car!" Linda challenged and started to run at a slow jog toward the parking lot.

"I've got the keys!" I called back and began my own slow, limping jog toward the car.

Although she had a head start, she was slowed by a patch of ice, and we both reached the passenger door at about the same time. I unlocked the door and opened it for her.

"Thank you," she said as she seated herself and wrapped her coat around her legs.

I closed the door in the most butlerlike fashion I could imagine and came to my side of the car. She had already unlocked my door. I got in and started the car. It took a little while to get heat this time.

"What kind of food would you like to eat?" I asked.

"I'm really not hungry enough for a fancy dinner at a German restaurant. I really would like to find a nice home-style one or maybe just a Denny's," she said.

"Well then, let's drive out to Lovers Lane Road and see what we can find," I answered.

"Not that I object, but isn't a bit early to go out there?"

That comment I made was a little joke I had with Jennifer because most Milwaukee residents knew Lovers Lane Road as Highway 100, which in its day was the western bypass around the greater city. Obviously, Linda was not in on the joke. I decided that I would have a little fun with that.

"We could go back to the lake front and watch the submarine races instead," I answered.

"Wouldn't it make more sense to go to my house?" She cuddled closer to me. "I could make it a lot more comfortable there."

I gave her a smile. "I like your offer, but I still want to check out Lovers Lane Road," I answered. I guess my smile must have given something away.

"What is on Lovers Lane Road that is so special? There must be something you are trying to surprise me with or you wouldn't look like

Sylvester the Cat with feathers in your mouth. I remember that look!" she answered. With that, she poked me in my ribs.

Now that brought back memories! Tweety Bird was one of her favorite comic book cartoon characters, and I was always Sylvester the Cat bothering her. I was prone to tease her, as most little boys in *like* tend to do. I would play tricks on her, and she would always know. She said my smile gave it away. What a memory she had to remember that!

"You'll just have to wait and see," I answered, making the motion and sounding like Sylvester spitting out feathers. "S-suffering s-succotash."

We were driving out National Avenue now and just looking at the Christmas decorations on some of the houses along the way. We passed through West Allis and the site of the old Allis Chalmers plant. There is a shopping center on the site now. We finally reached Highway 100. I made a left-hand turn onto it and spied a Denny's. The road sign said Highway 100. I made the necessary turns to get into Denny's parking lot.

After parking the car, we went inside. I gave the hostess my name, answered "nonsmoking," and waited with Linda to be seated. Even on a shopping night like this, the Saturday after Thanksgiving, when everyone should be eating at home, Denny's was full.

"Now tell me the joke!" she said, poking me in the ribs again.

"Highway 100 was always known as Lovers Lane Road when I lived here. I guess the joke is on me; they changed the sign." We both laughed.

"My offer still holds," she said.

"My second option still holds too," I answered.

"Tell me about a submarine race," she demanded.

"When I dated Jennifer—"

"I asked you not to mention her!" Linda interrupted with a hurt tone in her voice. "Please don't again. I want this to be my night!"

"I'm sorry," I said, and began again. "If you wanted to take a date to the lake to cuddle—we used to call it necking and petting—you wouldn't be so brash as to say, 'Let's go neck by the lake.' You would say, 'Let's go watch the submarine races!' Or, 'Let's go watch the grunion run!' It was a bit of a joke, as the fish could be doing anything under the water and you would never see, and I doubt that there were any submarines in

Lake Michigan during that time, but if there were, they would also be underwater."

"Oh! You men of the world," she answered, "always trying to pull one over on some unsuspecting girl!"

"Oh, the games people play then and now," I answered. After I said that, I thought it was probably in poor taste and was thinking about how to explain my way out of that when the hostess came to seat us.

The hostess led us to a table in the nonsmoking section. Linda began removing her scarf and then her coat. I stepped behind her to help her with her coat. I made my best effort to properly handle the chair to seat her. I laid her coat on the chair next to us and began to remove mine. I placed it on top of hers and then almost knocked my chair over as I tried to seat myself. So much for gallantry!

"You don't have to clown around for me," Linda said laughingly. "Now you have my undivided attention."

I guess she thought I did that on purpose. Well, the luck of the evening was going in my favor. "I always aim to please."

The waitress was there with two glasses of ice water and an order pad in her hand. "Can I get either of you coffee or a soda?" she asked.

"None for me," I replied. "The water is just what I need. Linda?"

"Water will do fine," she answered.

"Are you ready to order, or should I give you more time to think?" asked the waitress.

With that, we both looked at the menu and gave her our orders. She left to have them filled.

We just sat there and looked at each other across the table for the longest time. I had no idea what she was thinking. I was studying her features and more or less forming the mental picture I would carry in my mind when I would remember her in times to come. This was a fun time, a pseudo date, a time to remember, but it had to end. I will be in Atlanta. She will be at her home with her husband.

There is an old Scottish proverb that goes something like this: you're born cold and crying, you live your life in sadness, and you die alone. I may not have it quite right, but its meaning is paraphrased. I looked into her eyes. Their special color still had not changed from my first look at her in fourth-grade class. The gold color had left her hair, but the white with the gold tint paid tribute to what once was. Her other features were more mature, but were still as my memory had dictated they should be. I was looking at a mature woman, yet I saw also the ghost of the memory of how she was.

"What are your plans for next week?" she asked.

That broke my spell. "Ah...oh...ah, I guess when I get home Sunday night I will start looking through my mail and probably start returning customer calls first thing Monday morning," I answered.

"You promised to spend Sunday with me," she pleaded.

"Your husband will be coming home Sunday, won't he?" I asked.

A long silence broke the mood, as if I had again uttered a forbidden word.

"I want the whole day Sunday. Please stay. Your ticket is for Monday morning, and the car is rented 'til then. Please stay."

"I never could turn you down. I guess I can't now either. Only I feel our being together is so futile," I answered.

"So, what will you do on Tuesday when you are back at work?" she asked again.

I told her about my work and my company. I was involved in the art of selling and financing Capital Equipment. When the waitress brought the meal, we stopped talking and began to eat.

"Tell me about the letters you found in the old servants' quarters of your house?" I asked.

"As I said earlier, I found them in the hiding place in the baseboards. It wasn't obvious the boards were loose, but when I was trying to match the pattern of the wood, I pried at the boards in several places and found a number of letters and things.

"One was a short diary of an Irish girl named Mary McSomething. The last name was illegible due to deterioration of the paper. She was working off her passage to the New World. She described her daily routine and how she felt about it. She made entries every Sunday for nearly a year before things started to go badly for her.

"It all started when the seventeen-year-old son of the owner began to get fresh with her. She was only nineteen at the time, and he was very handsome. For the next six months, they became friendlier and friendlier. She was in fear of being found out, and he was threatening her with telling to force her to do as he demanded. She had almost finished her second year of servitude when she found out she was 'with child.' She then made entries until she began to show. That is when the diary entries stopped."

"Did you try to find public records that might have indicated where she went?" I asked.

"There is no record we could find to shed light on what could have happened to her," she replied.

"And there was no indication written in the diary of her intentions?"

"Obviously, her departure was abrupt, and she either had no time to get her diary or left it there on purpose."

"Could she have suffered so much shame that she killed herself?" I asked. "Did you check the obituaries in the paper of record for that time or even the local graveyards where she could have been buried?"

"We never considered that she might have died," she answered. "We thought she might have married and looked for those kinds of records. We found nothing. We might consider looking for an indication she might have died, either of an illness or by her own hand. That solution, though, is not one any of us on the historical board will pursue with happiness."

"It was just a thought. Life was brutal back then, and there was not a lot of forgiveness going around either, especially to immigrants," I replied. "I hope for the best in this case also."

As we continued to eat, we commented back and forth on some of the other less interesting notes left by the female servants of that time. We ate, we laughed, and we ate some more.

"Do you have kids?" It was the waitress asking as she stood by the table. "I mean, you are such a nice couple. You should have really great kids. You two just look so comfortable together." She was not more than a kid herself.

What to answer? The kid had paid us a compliment. I, the salesman, would have to answer, and again I was without words.

"Well, yes and no. They are all grown and moved away," was Linda's answer, "and we think they are very nice."

"That's great!" she said as she gathered up our plates. "Can I bring you any dessert?"

"Linda?" I asked, and she shook her head no. "None for me either, but thank you." She left the check and went away.

I looked at the check and left a healthy tip. I got up out of my chair, clowning a little just for the fun of it. I picked up Linda's coat, missing mine as it fell to the floor. I handed her the scarf and held the coat as she put her arms into the sleeves.

On the way out, I paid the cashier. While I was doing that, Linda visited the girl's room. I then went to visit the men's room. I found Linda waiting for me by the door when I returned. We walked out to the car arm in arm.

I held the door to the car for her to enter and closed it, as was becoming my habit. She unlocked my door, and that also seemed by now to be a habit.

"Where do you want to go now?" I asked. "This is your night!"

"You choose," she answered demurely.

"We can drive over to Lincoln Avenue, and I'll drive you through Greenfield Park. When we are there, we can even get out of the car and walk around the lagoon," I answered.

"Whatever you wish," she answered.

I drove us over to Greenfield Park. It was very pretty, with the streetlights illuminating the snow. It would have been a nice night to walk around the lagoon—not too cold and not too windy. As I parked by the curb, however, I looked over at the snow in front of the lagoon and saw the birds. That's right, birds! Ducks and geese, or maybe just geese. They were huddled together against the cold, but the snow from the curb to the lagoon for a great distance was covered in bird crap. The birds had taken the beach and any person not wanting to spend the rest of the night cleaning stuff from the bottom of his or her shoes would do well to stay in the car. Linda agreed.

The time was fast approaching 7:30 p.m.; the sun had set, but the light from the moon reflected from the snow gave the night an almost day-like quality. Still, I was feeling a little sleepy from my week of self-abuse as a deer hunter. "You do want to drive your car home from Janesville tonight, don't you?" I asked.

"Not unless you follow me home to make sure I make it safely," she answered with a coy smile on her face.

I knew I was hooked on that one. "Well then, we will head for Janesville and begin returning cars." A while back, I had studied a map of the southern Wisconsin expressway system and noticed I-39 from Hales Corners to Beloit. In my mind, that looked to be the best drive, and I could drive north on I-90 to the motel. I headed west out of the park to the street Lincoln Avenue teed into. I turned left and planned to get on I-39 somewhere around where that street crossed it. When I got on I-39, I drove toward Beloit.

During the ride on the somewhat deserted back road, Linda arranged herself so she was again laying her head on my shoulder. The faint light from the moon accented the silver in her hair, attracting my attention again to just how beautiful she looked.

"Tell me about your recovery from the accident," she said.

"You already know most of the story, and I really don't like to recount it," I answered.

She let the answer pass and asked, "Where do you plan to spend this Christmas?"

"I have nine days planned in San Antonio, TX. I reserved a room in the Holiday Inn on the Riverwalk. They normally have a very good celebration, and I can get lost in the crowds," I answered.

"Tell me about the Riverwalk," she said.

"It's not much really. The Bexar River was near the Alamo mission, and it curved and formed almost a loop in that area. When the city began to be built, it was built on both sides of the river, basically on the flood plain."

"Not very wise to do that," she commented.

"Later, because of flooding and flood control, a new channel was dug, connecting the river to bypass the part that looped through the city. The part that looped was then dammed off and made into a rather enjoyable lagoon-type park area. Later, the tourists found it, and now it is a great place to visit." I continued to describe the area and the things to do until we had reached the turn to put us on I-90 North.

At that point, Linda again said, "Tell me about your recovery from the burns you suffered in the accident."

"I guess the recovery was pretty good. I'm here with you," I answered.

"That's not what I want to hear. I saw you naked last nigh—"

"And you are still here with me today. You didn't retreat, you didn't run, and you didn't give me that horrified look. But now what?" I asked as I interrupted her.

"I saw you as you are, very scarred and misshapen. No, I didn't run. Was I supposed to? I looked at the scars and what is left of you. It didn't horrify me; it didn't turn me away. I can accept you as you are."

"You can say that as a friend. I was not trying to make love to you," I answered. "Everyone except my wife has been horrified and abandoned me immediately. My wife always looked away in horror, but she stayed until other things drove her away."

"I couldn't control what it did to them or your wife," Linda said as she held tightly to my arm. "I can control me. I will never look away. I can love you for whom and what you are, not how you look. I can even love you if there is no way you can physically make love to me."

"But loving me is not right! You are another man's wife! I can love you, but only from a distance. I will probably never love another, but I used to be able to control my loneliness. We made our decisions so long ago, and now they are set in concrete. I am free and lonely, but you are still as unobtainable as you were back before I moved from Edgerton."

"Peter. Oh, Peter," she began. "I was young. I was hurt. I was many things. It wasn't until after I had the children I realized what a mistake I had made. Marrying Mark was wrong, and we did it for the wrong reasons. After the barhopping, we had nothing in common. With the children, we were able to share in their lives, but we were never really together. As they grew up, we had nothing in common anymore. I was so lonely, but I remained a good wife.

"I think I still looked at you as my one true friend. I may have even felt love. I don't know. I wanted so much to find you. I had no idea if you were alive or dead. I only knew that it was your memory I was cherishing my whole life. Somehow, I knew you were still alive and one day would cross my path again. I believed that with all my heart. Once, I even tried to track you down through one of those services. That was how I found out your parents were dead. I never in my wildest dreams expected you to walk through the doors where I worked. You mentioned the old gang. It is no more. No one that ever had contact with you even knows any of my friends. Now I have found you, and my heart is yours for the taking."

"I lost a wife once. She chose to leave. It is not easy for a man to have that happen. I am certain that you have such a man who, over the years, has grown to be this close to you. I am certain that you still love him and deep in your heart could never decide to leave him," I said as her head lay on my shoulder.

"My man, as you called him, has not set foot in my bedroom for six years. I have not set foot in his for that same amount of time. He comes and goes as he pleases, although we do keep each other informed as to where we are. It is rare he eats what I cook, and I refuse to eat what he cooks. We got married for convenience, stayed married because of the boys, and now I only stay married because of the financial advantage," she explained.

"How did you arrive at the separate bedrooms?" I asked.

"He acquired a younger woman friend in Madison and has continued that relationship for the last seven years."

"You must have been devastated. How did you find out?"

"I was unaware for about a year. I thought because I was growing old he no longer was attracted to me, as he showed less and less interest in making love to me. I was told about her by a mutual friend, had it verified by a detective—"

"Did you confront him about this?" I interrupted.

"Not really. I just suggested he move into his own room. At that time, there was no economic advantage to divorce, and now he seems happy with the arrangement. I don't know if the boys know or not," she answered. "I've never said a thing to them, and they have not acted as if they know."

"What do you want to do now?" I asked.

"It is entirely up to you. I know you will do the right thing."

She did not make it an ultimatum. It was more a plea for me to do the right thing.

"There are things you do not know about me that should influence your decision," I proclaimed. "There is my physical condition, my business load, my almost constant travel, and my being set in my ways."

As I was mentioning all these considerations, she inched closer on the seat, undid her seatbelt, looked up into my face, and commanded, "Kiss me please!"

The road was clear and straight, the nearest car was a long way behind me, and I could see no reason not to do as she asked. I leaned over to kiss her. Some have called me dense. Others have called me slow to catch on when these situations present themselves. Tonight, I knew instinctively a kiss on the forehead would not cut it. I watched the road with one eye as our lips touched and her passion flowed to me. I tried to watch the road as I kissed back with the passion from my youth. The kiss was finally broken off when the wheels on the right side of the Sable began to rumble as they drove along the washboard warning strip at the edge of the road.

"Linda, if we do this again, we will be in the ditch!" I exclaimed. "Let's wait 'til we get to the motel parking lot, or at least off this highway before we do that again!"

"I'll just hug you then," she said as her grip tightened around my right arm.

"What are we going to do about your car?" I asked. I didn't want to spoil any plans she had for the night. On the other hand, the car belonged in her garage.

"Whatever you decide is okay with me," she answered.

"I think the prudent thing to do is for me to follow you in your car to your house like you suggested earlier."

"That would work out just fine," she answered with a coy smile on her face.

If I read that one right, she had some plan in her mind for me when we did get there. We were very close to the exit for the motel, so I began to slow the car. "Then it's settled. I'll follow you to your house. I think it would be a good idea, though, for us to stop and get gas before we make that trip."

I drove the Sable into the motel parking lot and over to where her car was parked. I helped her out of the Sable, and, as I was trying to be a gentleman and help her into her car, she again hugged me and found my lips with hers. This kiss was so intense it took my breath away, and had I not been leaning against her car, the dizziness it produced would have brought me to my knees.

"I'll clean the frost from the windshield if you'll start the car and begin warming it up," I said as I was trying to catch my breath. I got the scraper furnished with the Hertz rental car from inside of my car and went to scrape hers. The moonlight made the job of scraping easier, as I could see what I was doing. As I began to scrape the windshield, she started her car.

"That should be clean enough, at least until we get to a filling station," she said.

"I'll follow you, as you know your way around here much better than I do," I told her.

I got in my warm car and followed her as she led me out of the parking lot and onto Highway 14 West. Instead of turning up on I-90, she led me to Highway 26, where we turned right. There, where it crossed under I-90, were several gas stations. I followed her to the Shell station. When both cars were filled and the gasoline paid for, she led me up on I-90 North toward her home.

The drive to her house gave me time to calm down and begin to analyze what had happened. *First and foremost, it is up to me to do the right thing! What did that mean, the right thing? Am I to invite her to come and live with me? I never thought of her as that kind of girl, but she is a girl no longer! Am I supposed to come up with a plan? And then what about Mark? She is, after all is said and done, still his wife. How will his ego take this change? And yet, the right thing is for me to board an airplane and head back to Atlanta as fast as possible! The right thing for how I have lived my life is to leave this married woman to go back to her husband!*

I mulled these questions over and over in my mind, trying to seek the wisdom to find a reasonable solution; "the right thing," she had said. "You do the right thing." *The right thing by what definition?* All the unanswerable questions were going through my mind. *Do the right thing for me is one thing. The right thing for her seems to be another. I can't let her down! This may be a test! We will have to talk.*

As these things were bouncing around through my mind, we came to her road and then her house. She pulled her car into the garage. I pulled my car to the usual position across from the side door of the house. I turned the ignition off, pushed the light switch to off, and opened the door. There she stood beside the car in the moonlight, waiting for me to get out.

She took me by the hand and led me into the garage. She closed the garage door and took me by the hand in the sudden darkness up several steps through a door into the mudroom. The light from the moon shining through the windows into the kitchen made turning on that light unnecessary. She still had me by the hand as she led me into what had been the dining room two nights before.

Much later, I left her house, kissing her good-bye at the side door. Her parting words were, "Be here as close to 10:00 a.m. as possible." When I got into the Sable, I saw the picnic basket and the remains of the noon lunch still in the backseat. I made a mental note to give them to her the next day. I didn't get much thinking done on the drive back to the motel. I was too busy trying to stay awake!

Where Will You Be in Eight Months?

It is early Sunday night, and tonight I will try to sleep for a long winter's night, but considering what happened today, it may not happen in spite of the hours I have allotted. My excitement may make sleep impossible.

Tomorrow, I will be on the plane for Atlanta. My hunting trip will be done. I will have returned with the satisfaction that I got my deer. I will return with the expectation and the hope for what might be next July in Vancouver, BC, Canada.

XXXXX

This morning, I awakened to another sunny day that brightened my room and made me think I was back in the South. When I got out of bed and checked the time, it was only 8:30. That gave me a lot of time to get ready for today's visit to Linda. I showered and shaved. I splashed on some of that expensive aftershave lotion I use when I am selling on the road. I found it in the bottom of my suitcase the other day and decided now was the appropriate occasion to wear it. I dressed in my best slacks and shirt and wore a sweater over that for warmth under my thin, Atlanta-weight winter coat. Finally, I put my shoes on. I was headed out the door when the phone rang.

"Hello," I answered.

"By George, you are there!" It was John's voice on the phone, and he sounded surprised.

"Why do you sound so surprised to find me here?" I asked.

"I tried calling you last night, and the desk clerk said no one by that name was registered. Then I called your house and your housekeeper told me you would not be back until Monday late. Then I called Riley—"

"That must have been interesting!"

"Actually, it was. He filled me in about your week of hunting. How in blazes did you ever convince them you knew which end of the gun to point or even what you were doing?"

"I didn't think they ever really thought I knew what I was doing," I responded.

"Riley said you took the best shot any of them had seen in a long time and got your deer! He ribbed me about my first deer, when I cut the bladder and the dogs wouldn't even eat the meat! How in blazes did you gut that thing? I had planned to teach you how when we got our first!"

"Have you ever had the safety on your gun freeze in the safe position?" I asked innocently.

"No!" came his reply. "Why do you ask?

"Maybe I'll tell you sometime," I replied. "As to the gutting, I read the book pages I had Xeroxed at the Edgerton public library and actually was able to watch one of the guys do it to his deer a couple of days earlier. Some things I learn fast."

"One more question before I say good-bye. On the day you got the deer, what were you doing with your head hanging down on one side of the stand and your feet on the other? Riley said he looked around your stand after you left and couldn't determine if you were hurling, and you didn't seem hung over, sick, or anything like that. Were you looking for something you dropped?"

"It's a long story, John, and someday when we have the time and we are sitting down in comfortable chairs, I might even tell you about it," I answered, continuing the suspense.

"I'll have a hard time waiting for that story. By the way, how come you decided to stay the extra days and not go out and hunt with the guys?"

"I got my deer and decided to vacate the premises before I shot myself somewhere important," I replied. "By the way, do you know whatever happened to a Linda Swensen?"

"I don't know that I remember a Linda. Why do you ask?" he replied.

"I have been doing an awful lot of thinking on this trip, and in some ways, it probably was not wise for me to have come back," I answered.

"Yes, I guess your memories of the place were probably pretty traumatic," he replied. "It might have been a mistake to have asked you. I had some of my best memories there and for many years have enjoyed going back to hunt. By the way, did you get a chance to visit the Oats Bin?"

"You never mentioned that place," I replied with a chuckle in my voice.

"I was saving that as my little surprise," John answered.

"Didn't Riley tell you?" I asked.

"Okay, what did you do to Riley that he didn't tell me about?" John asked.

"Didn't pour a mug of beer over his head was all!" I laughed.

"If you would have been there, he would have told me!"

"He had his back to the bar," I replied with a laugh.

"I have to go or we will be late for late church. I'll see you when you get back down my way," John said as he hung up the phone.

I left my room and headed out of the lobby to the Sable. The weather was still cold, probably around twenty-five degrees, but the sun was causing the greenhouse effect in the car, and it was comfortable once I was inside. I looked at the clock and found I was at least a half hour late already and I hadn't stopped yet for my coffee and roll at the quick stop. I was at least forty-five minutes late entering the on ramp to I-90. Then I was behind a state trooper all the way to the 106 turnoff. *Better late than never*, I thought. I drove along slowly, my forward motion being hampered by my observing the speed limit.

Off and on during the night, I had awakened with that uneasy feeling about the relationship I now had with this *crush* from the past, this currently married lady. As I drove behind the state trooper, I had extra time to think again about what had to be done. *She wants me to take the initiative and decide what we should do, yet she is the married one and will be most affected by any decision I make. She is also in a marriage that, by her account, has been over for at least six years. This is really not right! She made a contract! But in this day and age, things are different. Jennifer made a contract, and where is she now?* The thoughts were still flying around in my mind when I drove into Linda's driveway. I turned the car around and parked it in the usual place. I got out and went to the side door of the house, as had become my custom.

She must have watched me come up the path and onto the porch, because when I reached the door, she opened it, immediately flung her arms around my neck, and buried her head in the front of my coat. She seemed to be shaking. It took me a minute, standing there in the draft of the open door, to figure out that she was crying.

Sensing something was wrong, I gave her a long, tender hug and asked, "What is the problem?"

She was silent as she slowly moved away from me and tried to blot her eyes with her hands. I slowly moved out of the way of the door and closed it to keep the cold outside.

I looked at Linda standing there, her makeup having been smeared by the tears. She stood there like some character from a Norman Rockwell painting, the picture of simple beauty. She was dressed in a black-pleated skirt and white blouse with three-quarter sleeves and a very wide collar. She had her string of pearls around her neck. She was wearing low-heeled black shoes that kind of resembled loafers and sheer nylon stockings. The sight was too much for me to just look at, so I went to her and hugged her again.

We stood in silence for a time until, finally, I backed away a little and took her by the hand. I led her to the kitchen table, pulled out a chair, and seated her, facing a corner of the table. I then went around the corner of the table and removed my coat, laying it out of the way on a chair by the table, and positioned a chair so as I sat on it I was facing her across the corner. I reached across the short distance that separated us and placed her hands in mine. As I sat facing her, holding her hands, I saw her wedding ring on the proper finger of the left hand and felt again the guilt of being with the wife of another. Knowing that he had rejected her still did not lessen that guilt. "What happened?"

"You were so late!"

"John called just as I was leaving my room. His call and other things on the highway delayed me," I answered.

"I was so afraid you wouldn't come when you weren't here by 10:00. I was worried that something—an auto accident, a fall, or some calamity—would keep you from me! Then when I didn't hear from you and you were so late I was afraid I had scared you away by being so bold last night," she confessed. "I was so afraid, and then you finally came, and I guess my emotions just got away from me. I was so happy and so relieved!"

"I should have called to tell you I was late," I answered. "It's just that I never expected you to worry."

"I have lived now for years with a man who has rejected me. Many things in my life are dreary and lonely, and I didn't want to be rejected by you. As the minutes passed, I was so afraid that something happened and you couldn't come, and then that you wouldn't come"—she sobbed—"that you would leave Janesville without even saying good-bye."

"I couldn't do that to you, today or any other day. I tried to say good-bye before my move to Detroit. I try to keep my word. Besides, yesterday was special to me, too. No woman has ever given so truly of herself as you did," I answered. "Please stop crying. We have a lot of things we have to talk about and try to settle today."

"Okay," she answered, still brushing tears from her face. By now, her makeup was pretty streaked, and her eyes were red.

"Let me ask you some questions," I began.

She made a motion to speak, and I placed my index finger slightly beneath the middle of her nose across the front of her lips and said, "Shh. Shh." I began again. "Who am I to you? Shh. Shh," I said again as she tried to speak. "Am I a memory, the answer to a prayer by a lonely woman, the manifestation of a dream, or an exciting interlude in your life? Shh. Shh. What are you to me, an awakening of a dormant dream; the answer to a wish made a million times to a million nameless stars; a bright moment in my existence; or the last attempt of a lonely old man to stave off, for a time, his ultimate loneliness? Shh. Shh.-These are the questions that we must address together. Last night was special in many ways, but you are still married. Where is the foundation that could make it permanent?"

We sat in deep thought, together, but apart, me rehashing in my mind again much of what I already gone over and over, again and again. Then my eyes looked to her left hand at the ring on that special finger. At the same time she, mysterious as ever, was sitting there looking back and forth at me and at her ring. I had no idea what was going through her mind as we continued to sit there.

"What is love?" she finally responded. "Is it a fleeting emotion, or is it a lasting understanding? Have I ever known love in my marriage? Mark has made love to me. I responded in like manner, but was I ever really attached to him? Obviously, his attachment to me never was permanent. In all my years with Mark, I never waited with the kind of excitement for him to come home that I have felt these last days waiting for you to arrive. Is that excitement real? How long will that excitement last?"

"Likewise, I have deep feelings for you. A memory of the companionship we once had, the desire to just be with you for no good reason, even a great loyalty to you. I gave all that up once. I buried it away and thought it forever gone, but it has surfaced. Yet, you wear that ring. That ring was your lifetime commitment to him, even when he didn't keep his to you. Even then, you never took the ring from your finger"

With a slow, deliberate motion, she slipped the ring from her finger and placed it on the table in between us. We both looked at what lay there, symbolizing the legal wall that had not moved. Then, slowly, she placed the index finger of her right hand next to the ring and pushed it from between us to another place on the table.

"Now the barrier is moved. Will that make a difference in how you feel about me?" she asked.

"You know deep down I believe I love you, and in some respects that feeling has stood the test of time. It has resurfaced and seems to be stronger than ever. The big question really comes down to whether I really know you and love you as you are or if I love the memory of who you were. Then the question becomes will this relationship stand the test of time? Taking away the ring removes the symbol of the barrier that separates us from ever finding out if our love is real or just an illusion."

"I love you and have for years. It has been an illusion, though, as I had no idea if you were even still alive. I guess you have been my dream. Thoughts of you and what might have been were my escape from the loneliness I have here. Your being here has given me the hope of rescue from this. I don't want to continue on in my present situation. I want to follow my dream. I want to follow where you lead and just be with you," she said as she moved my hands together and placed hers around them.

I looked across the table at her and tried to organize my thoughts and fears into some reasonably coherent response. "I want to be completely honest with you and tell you how I feel. I can say good-bye and walk away from your house today. I can go home and immerse myself totally in my work, and I will hurt. I will be lonely, sad, and maybe even depressed. I have been there before, when my hopes have been shattered. Actually, several times. I might get over it soon, or it might last until I die of old age. In any case, life will go on—"

"What are you telling me?" Linda nervously interrupted.

"Let me continue," I replied with a quiver in my voice. "Or I can go home and bring you with me. My business will require me to be working away from home often. You will be left alone in a strange city far from your family and friends. You will have as many new friends as you can find, and your family as it is will still be back here. You may suffer from loneliness. Your boys will get married, and there will be grandchildren. Someday, I will come home from a trip to find a note telling me you have gone back to visit and you don't know for how long. The weeks turn into months, and I can't find you to try to get you to return. I am a master of coping with this problem. It has happened before; my dreams have evaporated in the midst of a trip. I don't want it to happen again. The hurt on both sides is too great."

"But I will never do that!" came her swift, forceful reply.

"The gulf of time has been great. We don't really know each other. I might be stuck in some ruts unacceptable to you and you the same. You might compare what you have given up to what you have and decide you made a bad mistake. The dream could have been more exciting than the reality. The relationship might not be there," I concluded.

Linda raised her voice and said, "Would you be quiet long enough for me to defend myself? Have you spent so much time thinking of the negatives that you fail to see me? Be quiet and listen! Granted, you have been hurt. You have had some rough times. Those women were not me! I am not like that. My life has been empty after Mark and I moved out and left the boys. The boys were my life. I waited for Mark to come home years ago. It never happened. I will wait for you to come home no matter how long you take." She stopped talking to catch her breath and then continued. "My love is something I have unconditionally given. Don't you think I have been hurt too? I guess my options have been more limited in such a small town. Don't question my ability to keep my word or my staying power please!"

"I wasn't trying to do that," I responded defensibly. "I wanted only to point out the inherent problems we could face if we rushed into some action here. I told you earlier that these were my fears. I wasn't making predictions!"

"Let me tell you my fears then," Linda forcefully replied as she raised her voice.

"My biggest fear is you will leave and I will lose you for the second time. You have aged, but I recognize in you the man that the boy I wanted has become. You haven't changed! The same things still drive you! I haven't seen you in all these years, yet you are the same person, just a little larger and a little older and maybe more stubborn! Hopefully, you are not as dense as you once were and can see what is being offered to you!"

"I see what is offered, and I like what I see. I don't want to make a mistake, though, that costs both of us. If you stay here with Mark, you have security, and who knows; Mark may someday recognize what it is he has and come back. If you come with me and things don't work out, you have burned all your bridges. For a young person to gamble like that is expected. For an older person to give up their security is a risk few can afford to," I replied.

We sat across from each other, Linda holding my large hands tightly in her small hands for a long time. The barrel of worms was crawling again through my brain.

"This is getting us nowhere. Would you like to go somewhere or do something? We still have the rest of this day," I said.

"Can we go back to Milwaukee? I would like to walk through one of the malls," she answered.

"Brookfield Square Mall is pretty close. The Christmas decorations will all be up, and the crowds should be thinner than yesterday. It should be nice. By the way, when should Mark be coming home?"

"I didn't tell you? Oh! I guess not. He called this morning about 9:00. He said the boys will be driving back today, but he plans to hunt and drive back late tonight directly to work. I won't see him until tomorrow night," she stated in a disgusted manner.

"I hope he gets one today then," I answered.

She continued as if she didn't hear me. "Translated, that means as soon as the boys are a half hour down the road, he will get in the car and drive to her apartment in Madison to spend the night. Sometimes, I wish he would just come right out and say it! I hate all these damnable lies he keeps telling!"

I picked up my coat from the chair where I had placed it. As I was putting it on, I noticed the ring was gone from where it had been on the table. This was the first time I had ever heard her use any language that was that harsh. I wonder how she has put up with this all these years. Linda had gone through the door into the other part of the house. When she returned, her makeup was repaired. She had retrieved her coat from a closet somewhere and was about to put it on when I came over to help.

As I reached for the coat, she said, "I can get this okay, but if you want to help, just hold it at that shoulder while I adjust my sleeve."

As she turned her head, I could see the bruising from the other night, the slight lump and the stitches that were still there. "How does your head feel?" I asked.

"Still a little tender," she replied.

We went out of the house, and as we were walking to the car, I commented, "I've never seen you lock your house."

"There is a small deadbolt on the door that locks itself when the door is closed, but out here anyone who wants to can get in, and there seems to be no way to protect against that. We just don't keep anything we can't afford to lose in the house," came her answer.

When we got to the car door, I opened it for her and helped her in. "The sun sure has made it warm in here," I said, trying to fill the silence with small talk.

It seemed since she told me about Mark, her mood had become dark, and I wanted so much to brighten up again. I closed her door and went around to my side of the Sable. I got in, closed my door, and started the motor. She immediately reached with her left hand to tune the radio. That was when I noticed her ring finger no longer had the gold band in place. Where it had been there was a groove in the skin much lighter in color than the rest of the finger, somehow giving the impression the finger itself were naked. I had not shifted the car into gear yet, and I guess my sudden lack of attention to driving gave her time to notice me starring at her naked finger. As I looked up, she caught my gaze and gave me a big confident smile. As I leaned toward her, she leaned toward me, and as our lips were about to meet for a kiss, the static electricity that follows cold weather sparked between our lips. I can state absolutely that that was the most electrifying kiss I ever had. Surprisingly, neither of us flinched in the slightest.

Linda had chosen well when she tuned the radio. She had tuned in a local station that played a version of elevator music and was very good background for the insignificant banter that took place in the car as we drove toward Milwaukee. Should I describe the route that we took, I would only bore you, as it was almost exactly the same as it was the last times. The only deviation, though, was to skip the bypass and go through the drive-through at the McDonald's in Fort Atkinson for two Big Macs and a Coke to share. After all that kissing, who worried about a few germs on the straw? Also, I kind of liked the taste of her lipstick on the straw, as that flavor had been lacking from my taste buds since Jennifer.

It was a little after 1:00 p.m. when we reached the Brookfield Square Mall. Although it was early on Sunday, the mall parking lot was still full. We drove around and jousted for parking spaces with other shoppers for about half an hour. Finally, I got lucky in the north parking lot. Just as someone was backing out of a spot, I was able to muscle the Sable into it ahead of a large, old Pontiac that suddenly seemed too large to fit. It was a long walk, but we finally entered the mall. The Christmas decorations were beautiful. They were what really set the festive atmosphere for the weekend after Thanksgiving.

We walked around from store to store, looking at things and buying little. Eventually, were at a high-end jewelry store window. Visible in the window display was a diamond pendant that caught her eye. We joked about Liz Taylor and the things she wore to the movie openings. We both had seen the movie *Cleopatra* and remembered the jewelry she wore to the grand opening. We joked about the need for jewelry to enhance the beauty of a lovely lady. The result was for us to enter the store and begin looking at things to be worn around the neck.

I have not had much experience with jewelry store salespeople, but I found them to be very observant. The pleasantries of the day were exchanged. The salesman first looked at me and then at Linda's bare ring finger. "And what can I do for you today?" he asked, somewhat addressing me.

"Nothing in particular," answered Linda, the annoyance of having been asked that question sounding through her answer.

The salesman stood there for a moment, assessing the situation, and then remarked, "If there is anything you need, please ask me, and I will be happy to help you."

Linda turned and started toward the door. I followed, walking fast to catch up. As we were exiting together, walking out the door, she turned toward me and said, "I was so embarrassed with him looking at my ring finger and asking that question. I suppose I shouldn't have let it bother me, but the ring mark on the finger is so obvious!"

"Only to you and the salesmen in jewelry stores," I answered. "By the way, what did you do with your ring?"

"I sent a message!" she answered in an icy voice. "I placed a rubber band through it and hung it on the doorknob to Mark's room."

I mulled that over in my mind for a while, not knowing how to respond. In my heart of hearts, I was elated. My practical side, though, had another reaction, more of fear balanced against excitement. Obviously, Linda had turned a corner in her life and was now beginning to act to control it. Now it was my turn to say the right words to her and do the right thing to follow through on what must be perceived by her as the right response. What exactly was the right response? What was it she expected me to say?

"Is there any more of the mall you want to see?" I asked, trying to break the silence.

"No. I think I have seen all I care to," she answered. "Why don't you take me home?"

I turned and, taking her hand, led the way toward the south exit. It was the wrong way to find the Sable, but it was in the direction of the mall Christmas tree. There were some benches and places to sit around the tree for those tired shoppers who just wanted to relax in the atmosphere created there. When we got to the benches, I was able to spot one that was unoccupied. I motioned for her to sit and then sat beside her.

"Linda, what do you expect Mark to do when he finds that ring hanging on the door knob? How will he react? Will you be safe?"

"It may take him a week to notice it there. He will probably notice it is not on my finger first. Then, if he does notice it, he may respond by asking me what I am planning to do. He may just ignore the whole thing as if it didn't happen. I probably will have to end up telling him to look at the door knob!"

"Do you think he will try to make up with you, to recognize what it is he is losing, to try to win you back?" I asked.

"I expect he will go the opposite way and just move to Madison," she responded.

"You will be safe?" I asked.

"I have no fear. I believe he will grant an uncontested divorce."

"In that case, what will you do?" My words were not coming out right. "Would you consider...would it be possible for you to come to Atlanta to start over?"

My words were still not coming out the way I wanted them to.

"I'm still not getting this right! Would you consider..." I now moved from the bench to kneel on my right knee. I looked up at her and asked, "Would you allow me to court you, with marriage as the objective?"

"Would you even have to ask that question after last night?" she asked, sounding a little peeved.

"I asked that question because I didn't want to read things into your words or your actions that you didn't mean. I think you can call that a proposal. Yes, that is a proposal! It is difficult and out of place for me to ask because you are not free to accept, and I don't want to consider myself responsible for you taking your action. I do wish to know, however, if and when you do get that divorce."

She sat there looking at me still on one knee. She didn't speak; she just looked at me, then at the tree, then back at me, and shook her head.

I got up from in front of the bench, took her by the hand to help her up, and, hand in hand, we headed for the correct exit to find the Sable. As we were walking through the door going out, one of the people walking out ahead of us dropped a piece of important-looking paper on the floor. I bent to retrieve it to return it to the person. Upon examination of the paper, though, I found it was an advertisement for a restaurant featuring organ music.

Now, as we walked to the car in silence, holding hands, I began thinking that a nice, romantic restaurant with organ music in the background would probably be a great way to top off the afternoon. I glanced at the hours listed on the front and noted that on Sunday they were open from 4:00 p.m. to later than I wanted to stay. I looked at the address and found this place was located on Highway 100 on the way to Hales Corners. I began to plan.

I helped Linda into the car, and, again, she unlocked the door for me. I started the car and headed east on Bluemound Road toward Highway 100. Linda had no idea which direction was which and had no way of knowing I was headed the wrong direction. That way I could surprise her with this romantic place I had just found. Maybe after my Christmas tree bench debacle this would recreate the mood I was looking for. Luckily, I made no promises to Linda about it and therefore was not embarrassed by what we found.

As we drove south on Highway 100, I suggested we find someplace to eat, as it was getting late and the Big Mac wasn't lasting all that long. She heartily agreed, and I told her I would stop someplace. I drove the car into the parking lot for the Organ Piper Pizza Restaurant and Music Palace.

The only problem with the facility was it in no way resembled a palace. It looked as though it could be a warehouse with the facade of an Italian farmhouse! The entrance was on the south side of the building, and if I hadn't been looking for it, I would have never noticed where it was. Either it was early, about 5:30 p.m. and the crowd had not arrived yet, or the place didn't attract many people. The bottom line was that I was able to get a good parking place on this day of heavy shopping. I parked the car, was a gentleman with the passenger door, and, with Linda beside me, went through the entrance doors.

I expected to find an electronic organ discretely situated in a dimly lit corner playing elevator music for people sitting at candlelit tables and in candlelit booths. What I found was a large room with a long bar on one end. Across from the entrance on a raised dais was placed the console for the largest Kimball Theater Organ I had ever seen! On the wall behind the console were two 8'x10' windows displaying the ranks of twenty-seven sets of organ pipes. Above the windows were the two 8'x12' shuttered windows that controlled the volume of the sound emanating from the pipe room. On the walls and ceiling were placed various drums, cymbals, chimes, and other instruments critical to producing realistic sounds for silent movies. My candlelit tables turned out to be long tables with chairs on both sides. The booths were placed against one wall. There were no candles.

My romantic pizza palace turned out to be a place for family birthday parties and such. The procedure was to order the pizza you wanted from a corner of the bar. When the number on the ticket given you when you paid was lighted on the panel over the bar, you went up and claimed your meal. We were here, and I decided to make the best of it. This turned out to be a very good decision.

We chose a table, and I went to the counter to order a pizza and some beer. As I brought the beer back to the table, along with the receipt showing the number to watch for, a man dressed in a white shirt and black trousers mounted the dais and approached the organ. He limbered up and began playing requests from the floor. His first set was western songs. Then he played Disney favorites. He played music from romantic movies, followed by songs about trains. Each of these songs required the use of many of the extra sound effects that seventy years ago were necessary in any theater showing silent films. The performance was breathtaking.

Finally, our number came up. I brought the pizza back to the table and found it to be very tasty and not at all greasy. I could tell by the smile on Linda's face she was having a good time. We stayed for a while, listening to the beautiful organ music performed by one who must have been a master of the craft. Eventually, the time came when we had to leave.

We got in the car and headed back for her house. Nothing was said until we had driven past the St. John's Military Academy exit on I-94. She had not answered my strange proposal. She had not said no, but in her situation, she was not in a position to say yes either. If you spend a lot of time around salesmen, you will find silence is something they just can't stand. Someone has to speak, even if it turns out to be them.

"Until you decide about a divorce and how you will handle Mark, I don't believe it would be wise for us to be together. I don't think we can even communicate back and forth. We both have some things from our past that must be attended to before we can start to communicate and build a good relationship," I stated as I began to prepare myself for the seriousness of the situation and a "no" answer from her.

"I think you are right about the getting together, but I want to have your Atlanta address so I can at least find you when this is over," answered Linda.

"Can I take that as a tentative yes answer to my question to you at the Christmas tree?" I quietly asked.

"The ring is no longer on my finger. You can take that as a positive sign. I am sorry to not have said yes. This is all happening so fast. Until the divorce papers are official, I can't say yes."

"I accept that as a yes. I also have things to do to prepare for your being with me. I want to put my business affairs in order so my work will not cause me to steal valuable time away from you. If I must travel, I want you to come with me. It will take some doing, but I will move the business from the house and begin to live as a normal person again," I promised.

"Won't that affect your income? If you don't travel and don't sell, what will you live on?" she asked, looking serious.

"Believe me, my years of selling have been good to me. I can retire, and we will be able to live quite well from my savings. Any income from the business will be extra. How long will it take for you to get your situation settled?"

"I should have the papers all signed and the property settled by the end of June."

"Then let's plan to meet on July first. You name the place."

"That's a good date. I like that! I will have everything completed by then. Where can we meet? You have been to so many places. You choose," she excitedly said.

"You could come to Atlanta, or I could come to Edgerton. I am open to any suggestion."

"I want it to be somewhere far from here. I want it to be romantic. I want it to be somewhere out of a dream!"

I drove in silence for a while, trying to think of a romantic place to meet. *It could be Milwaukee. Then again, it could be Atlanta, or Chicago, or even*

Detroit, but those were all places I am familiar with. Yesterday, when Jennifer's name came up, she became upset. The place must be new to both of us. The place must be out of a dream.

"I'm thinking of someplace neither of us has ever been. I have always wanted to go there. You will need your passport and the faith to get on an airplane to meet me on July first at the airport in Vancouver, BC, Canada. I will make all the arrangements. I will even find a way to send you a round-trip ticket."

She didn't say a word. She just moved as close as she could get while still seat-belted in the Sable and hugged my arm. We drove in silence back to her house. When we arrived, I parked the car in the usual spot, got out, cleaned up the picnic basket and other things from the back seat of the Sable, went to the door on her side, and helped her out of the car. We walked arm in arm up the steps and across the porch to the side door leading into the kitchen. She hadn't locked it, so we went right in. I placed the picnic basket on the table and turned to leave.

"Where are you going? Take your coat off, and stay a while," she said.

"I must say good-bye and leave," I stated as I headed for the door.

"Please, won't you take your coat off and stay a while?" she pleaded.

"Linda, we have made our plans. We each know what it is that we must do. You know how I feel about you; I love you. You are in my heart. If I stay, I may not want to leave. We made plans to meet. I must go!" With that, I put my arms around her and gave her a good-bye hug. She found my lips, and we clung together for some time. I opened the door, feeling lightheaded from her perfume, and walked out into the cold night.

"I'll be there! I'll be there! Don't lose hope!" she shouted as I went to the car.

The drive back to Janesville was uneventful. I stopped for a Coke, but my excitement level was high, and I really didn't need the caffeine in it.

EPILOGUE

The next day, I boarded my flight, and Delta flew me home to begin to put my new plans into action. I had so much to do. I began to make plans on the back of the Delta boarding envelope.

Step number one: reassess my business.

Step number two: research Vancouver, British Columbia, Canada.

Step number three:—

But step three was interrupted by thoughts of Linda.

www.ingramcontent.com/pod-product-compliance
Lightning Source LLC
Chambersburg PA
CBHW070400200726
48294CB00003B/1021

* 9 7 8 1 9 6 1 4 1 6 0 0 0 *